Strategy in Practice

Study in Practice

Strategy in Practice

A Practitioner's Guide to Strategic Thinking

Second Edition

George Tovstiga

A John Wiley and Sons, Ltd, Publication

Contents

Preface to the First Edition

S trategy is still a source of contention in most organizations. It seems that since the beginning of time man has associated strategy with mystery and esoteric rituals restricted to only an enlightened inner circle. The ancient Greeks consulted their oracle at Delphi for guidance before moving into battle. Indeed, in preparing for the historic battle at Salamis in 480 BC that pitted the Greek coalition against the might of Xerxes' fearsome Persian army it took the persuasive and cunning "vision" of the Athenian *strategoi* (general) Themistocles, commander of the Greek allied navy, to provide an interpretation of the oracle that ultimately encouraged the Greeks to stay and fight in the face of almost certain defeat against the Persian army. Some had interpreted the oracle's sign to predict defeat. Themistocles skillfully and convincingly interpreted the oracle's omen to mean victory. Little, of course, could he or his Greek compatriots have appreciated the historical significance of their great victory in that battle.[1]

Many managers today still seek out their "oracles" when faced with strategic decision making. The modern manager's oracle often takes on the form of endless reams of essentially meaningless data generated by management information systems. Many managers find solace in numbers, just as the early Greeks did in the Delphian oracle's signs.

---

[1] Greene, R. (2006) *The 33 Strategies of War*, London: Profile Books.

Strategy need not be enigmatic. It need not be a mystical codex with seven seals. Good strategy is about clarity of thinking; of balancing insight based on well-founded intuition with rational analysis – particularly in the face of incomplete information and complex circumstances. Strategy is practiced in social contexts; that is to say, in organizations and their competitive environments. Admittedly, these represent ambiguous contexts that often defy rational analysis. Andrew Lo of MIT's School of Management has remarked that while in the physical sciences three laws can explain 99% of behavior, 99 laws in finance can at best explain only 3% of the behavior.[2] The latter can be argued for the social sciences in general. However, while the context in which strategy is practiced is complex and fraught with ambiguity, the basic premise of this book is that how we approach strategy need not be. In this book we develop an approach to strategy that seeks to fulfill that purpose. An underpinning element of this approach is the strategic thinking process that leads to the generation of strategically relevant insight, even in highly ambiguous and complex competitive contexts.

This book builds on several relatively simple assumptions. The first is that strategy is a practice discipline. While this extends to the field of management science in general, it is arguably in the strategy area that "getting it wrong" leads to the more serious consequences. Strategy attains meaning only in the practice field; indeed, some strategy thinkers even go so far as to suggest that strategy attains meaning only in the retrospective; that is, after the fact. Strategy may look impressive on paper, but it is in the practice field that it fulfills its ultimate purpose. While this may seem readily apparent to any military commander, it is not necessarily what the strategic management literature would lead us to believe. Second, strategy is not only about rational analysis and the models that support the analysis. No doubt, analysis is important in strategy. Indeed, as will be argued in this book, appropriately selected frameworks of analysis can generate a lot of useful insight. But as we will see, analysis is

---

[2] *The Economist*, Schumpeter – The Pedagogy of the Privileged (26 September 2009).

only one of several inputs to the strategic thinking process. Intuition, reflection and above all a predisposition for experimentation and learning are its other important constituents.

This book is about strategy in practice. It draws on strategy theory and current thinking in the field of strategic management. However, this book is written with the practitioner of strategy in mind – the manager who faces strategic decision making in everyday management practice. This is where strategy has the potential for making a difference in the business outcome of a firm. In my experience, both as management practitioner and consultant, this is where we often still find substantial gaps in the understanding of even very basic strategy concepts in firms. Managers typically have difficulty in knowing where to begin with strategy. Of those who do succeed in getting started, many quickly get bogged down in the maze of strategic analysis. This book seeks to address those gaps in understanding strategy; it aims to provide the strategy practitioner with a balanced compendium consisting of essential theory and pragmatic, practitioner insight. The strategic thinking approach that forms the core theme of this book delineates the path through the strategy forest.

Setting the right strategy is arguably the most critical managerial challenge facing a firm. Strategy is about making appropriate choices about *why*, *where* and *how* to compete. Decisions of this type are invariably being made under conditions of incomplete information in increasingly complex contexts. This doesn't make the task any easier. It does, however, reflect the reality of the complex, fast-changing and messy real world we compete in. In that context, strategy is first and foremost about *being different* and *doing things differently* in deliberate response to opportunities in the firm's external competitive environment. This response invariably takes on the form of creating and delivering a superior value offering to the market. However, strategy might also have an inward focus; it might also be thought about as seeking and achieving competitive advantage through differentiation in the strategic (re-)positioning of the firm. This might require a realignment of resources and capabilities to better fit changing circumstances in the external market environment.

Good strategy, whatever its pretext, demands astute and discerning insight – strategic insight which is grounded in a suitably balanced mixture of rational analysis, intuition, healthy skepticism, reflected experience, and the willingness and ability to continually challenge the prevailing logic and paradigms. In this book we explore the strategic thinking process which leads to strategic insight. This may seem a questionable proposition – a systematic approach to understanding a complex context? No doubt, competitive contexts are highly complex. Firms' external competitive environments are continually changing; internal organizational contexts are no less complex. Complexity, we know, inherently defies structure and order.

Why then a book about anything even remotely related to *structure* given the messy real world we are competing in? In this book we clearly differentiate between a firm's reality marked by complex and changing contexts and an appropriate *response* on the part of the firm to that reality. The former, the firm obviously can neither influence nor impose structure onto. The latter, however, clearly lies within the firm's realm of strategic choices. Strategy is about clarity of thinking; about making appropriate choices under conditions of incomplete information. Strategic thinking can be a powerful means to that end.

The strategic thinking approach developed in this book does not seek to achieve simplification of the firm's complex competitive context; rather, it seeks to bring structure to the *thinking* that allows managers not to lose sight of the wood for the trees. Good structured thinking begins with asking the *right* strategic questions – those that really have potential to make a difference to the firm's ability to compete in its markets. There might be numerous questions on a manager's plate, but in reality only relatively few of these have potential for really making a difference to a business's competitive situation. Managers will want to ensure that they are indeed focusing on the few high priority issues. Strategic thinking also continually challenges the prevailing business logic. It seeks to establish relevant insights and to understand these in their current strategic context. Insight ultimately leads to the emergence of patterns that reflect the firm's competitive landscape. Though inevitably incomplete and spotty, this level of granularity is often the best there is available. The good news in all of this is that the firm's competitors are no better off in this regard.

Arguably, strategic thinking leading to an insight-driven approach to strategy is an increasingly critical strategic capability enabling those firms that have acquired skill and acumen in its application to recognize and act on opportunities faster than their competitors; alternatively, it can help to avert situations that might prove to be detrimental to the firms' competitive position. Hence, there is a lot at stake. The purpose of this book is to provide a relatively accessible guide toward achieving mastery of this important skill.

The strategic thinking process developed and discussed in this book represents an accumulation of insights, experiences and reflections that have evolved as a result of my various roles over the years as management practitioner in industry, as strategy consultant and as professor of strategy. This book represents a summary of the insights distilled from experiences gained wearing these various hats both in the practice field and in academia. Boxed inserts throughout the book under the heading "*Strategy in Practice*" underscore the pragmatic emphasis on strategy. These provide practical insights and suggestions for applying the key notions and concepts discussed in the respective chapters.

There is little in this book that is *really* new. It would be equally pretentious to assume that a book of this brevity can exhaustively deal with strategy in its breadth. The focus of this book is on the front end of the strategy process; it is about setting the right strategic direction from the outset. To that end, this book does purport to make a unique contribution; its aim is to provoke a new and different approach to thinking about strategy.

In compiling the book, I have poached without remorse ideas and thinking put forward by fellow scholars. I am particularly indebted to former colleagues in industry and consulting, current colleagues in academia, my MBA and doctoral students. Particular mention must go to those at Bayer, ABB, Arthur D. Little, Henley Business School, the Private Hochschule Wirtschaft (PHW) in Zurich, Switzerland, and the University of St. Gallen, Switzerland. This book is as much a tribute to their generosity of spirit in sharing insights and experiences as it is to their relentless challenging of my thinking both in the practice field and classroom, respectively.

I am particularly grateful to several individuals who have contributed directly to the book. I am indebted to the following for their reviews of the manuscript, valuable feedback and endorsement: Professor Peter Lorange, Lorange Institute of Business Zurich (Switzerland); Leif Bergman, Managing Director of Henley Nordic (Denmark); David Wright, MD of AllCloud Networks and formerly a Strategy Director and Business Vice President at Hewlett Packard; Professor John McGee, Warwick University (UK); and Professor David Collis, Harvard Business School (USA). Further, I am grateful to Rosemary Nixon, Senior Commissioning Editor at John Wiley & Sons, for her unwavering support from the outset. Last, but by no means least, I am indebted to my wife, Heidi, for her meticulous scrutiny of several versions of the book's manuscript, and for engaging and challenging discussions on its content as it evolved.

I am grateful to all. It has been a great learning journey and I look forward to sharing some of the insights that have emerged with you in this book.

George Tovstiga
Henley-on-Thames
March 2010

Preface to the Second Edition

The need for clarity and structure in strategic thinking is greater than ever. Since publication of the first edition of this book, companies are facing ever greater challenges in a global economy marked by widespread uncertainty. New worries triggered by the Euro crisis have driven business confidence levels to unprecedented depths. Indeed, there is no end to the recession in sight as the threat of a "triple dip" recession in the foreseeable future appears ever more probable.[3] More than ever, firms are seeking new ways to approach their strategy; if not to achieve strategic growth, then to counter threats with more effective defensive strategies. Strategy, the way we know it, appears to have arrived at an evolutionary crossroads. The current economic crisis has introduced several important changes to the way in which we think about strategy.

The first has to do with our fundamental understanding of competitiveness, the firm's *"right to win"*. This has been defined as the ability of the firm to engage in its competitive markets with a better-than-average chance of achieving success – not

---

[3] Not all geographic areas are equally affected, of course; talk of a possible "triple-dip" recession is currently making its rounds primarily in the UK; see, for example, Groom, B. (2012) Companies to Cut Investment and Hiring, *Financial Times* (9 July 2012).

just in the short term, but consistently. This is being challenged as never before.[4]

Second, the notion of *"sustainable"* competitive advantage, while still conceptually interesting, is being seriously challenged in the practice field. Traditionally, the achievement of "sustainable" advantage has been the Holy Grail in strategy. Increasingly, however, firms are finding themselves pursuing not "sustainable" competitive advantage, but punctuated situations of *"unsustainable temporary"* advantage. Once achieved, these position the firm favorably only until the competition has caught up or markets have moved on – at which point the search for new advantage continues.[5] If anything, this new mantra has heightened the awareness that firms' strategy increasingly revolves around gaining relevant insight, rapid experimentation and evolutionary learning.[6] Kelly's[7] prescient assertion of firms engaging in ever more frequent cycles of *"find, nurture, destroy"* resonates closely to what we are, indeed, experiencing in the practice field.

This second edition of *Strategy in Practice* pursues the same purpose as its earlier edition: it seeks to provide the practitioner of strategy with a compendium that balances current thinking in the field of strategic management and pragmatic guidance for putting that thinking to practice.

This new edition, however, substantially extends the section on strategic sense making and analysis. Following on an introductory chapter on strategic analysis, two new chapters have been added; these elaborate on *high-level* and *supporting-level* strategic analyses. The distinction between the two levels of analysis

---

[4] Mainardi, C. and Kleiner, A. (2010) The Right to Win, *Strategy + Business* (Booz&Co), Issue 61 (Winter 2010).
[5] Stern, S. (2010) Get Your Strategy Right Now before the Dust Settles, *Financial Times* (21 July 2009).
[6] McGrath, R.G. (2010) Business Models: A Discovery Driven Approach, *Long Range Planning*, Vol. 43, pp. 247–261.
[7] Kelly, K. (1997) The New Rules of the New Economy: Twelve Dependable Principles for Thriving in a Turbulent World, *Wired*, September 1997.

is critical to strategic sense making and thinking; it is also a unique contribution of this book to the current thinking in strategic analysis. The *unique competing space* concept and analysis framework, a unique contribution introduced in the first edition, is also dealt with much more thoroughly in one of the new chapters (Chapter 5). Finally, this new edition of *Strategy in Practice* introduces some practical exercises in Appendices A and B for putting the thinking, concepts and frameworks introduced throughout the book into practice. These exercises have been used effectively in Executive Strategy seminar workshops around the world, and in consultancy work with both small start-ups as well as multinational firms.

I am sincerely grateful to fellow scholars, management practitioners and MBA students around the world whose generous feedback and suggestions on the first edition have contributed directly to this new edition. I am particularly indebted to my Henley DBA research associates, Henning Grossmann and Jacob Bruun-Jensen, for engaging discourse on a number of the key themes and concepts elaborated on in this edition; these have contributed significantly to their advancement. Further, I am grateful to Rosemary Nixon, Senior Commissioning Editor at John Wiley & Sons, for her continuing support for this edition.

Lastly, but by no means least, I am once again indebted to my wife, Heidi, for her careful scrutiny of the manuscript of this second edition, and for her numerous invaluable suggestions for clarification and structuring of its content.

The learning journey continues; with this second edition I look forward to sharing new insights and learning with you.

George Tovstiga
Henley-on-Thames
August 2012

About the Author

George Tovstiga is Professor of Strategy and Innovation Management at Henley Business School at the University of Reading where he is Director of the Henley Executive Strategy Programme and Lead Tutor for Strategic Management in Henley's MBA programmes. He teaches, researches and consults in the areas of strategy and innovation management. George has extensive international experience as management educator, industry management practitioner (including Xerox Research in Canada, Bayer AG in Germany and ABB Ltd in Switzerland), author and consultant. Prior to joining Henley, George consulted for Arthur D. Little (Switzerland) Ltd's Strategic Growth and Innovation Practice. He is a consultant to a number of multinationals in the area of strategy and has published extensively in this area.

CHAPTER 1

Introduction to Strategy in Practice and Strategic Thinking

It is important to remember that no one has ever seen a strategy or touched one; every strategy is an invention, a figment of someone's imagination . . .

—Henry Mintzberg

IN THIS INTRODUCTORY CHAPTER, WE . . .

- define and explore some fundamental notions related to strategy and the practice of strategy;
- review and frame some of the key problems and issues contributing to the ongoing dilemma managers face with strategy;
- introduce strategic thinking in the context of strategy in practice;

- reflect on the differences between strategy *in* practice and strategy *as* practice; examine *strategic planning* in the context of strategy in practice and strategic thinking;
- introduce the strategic thinking roadmap; briefly outline the subsequent chapters of this book that are structured around the strategic thinking process;
- close with some caveats and useful pointers on strategy in practice.

Strategy: A Persistent Dilemma

Strategy – is it really a figment of someone's imagination? One would hardly come to that conclusion judging by the popularity of the word in the business media. Scarcely any business word is invoked more frequently and with greater fervor. Business leaders take great pride in referring to "their strategy". A simple search of the *Financial Times* online (*FT.com*) for the period of the first two quarters of 2012 reveals that the word "strategy" comes up 4,137 times. The term is being used; in fact, it is being used a lot.

Yet many business leaders have difficulty articulating their strategy. Ask a business leader to explain their organization's strategy in simple terms; for example, how it sets them apart from their competitors. After all, do we not teach our MBA students that strategy is about being *different*? More often than not, however, this simple question elicits an evasive response. The sobering reality is that most business leaders cannot articulate their organization's strategy in a simple, compelling way. This is worrisome when considering that these are the people who not only view themselves as the chief strategist of their organization, but indeed, *are* responsible for the strategic course of their company.

Although business leaders often see themselves as the architects of their organization's strategy, many rather quickly lose sight of the wood for the trees when it comes to strategy. They are quickly baffled, if not by the jargon then by not knowing how to approach strategy in the first place. Surely, this cannot be for lack of "cutting edge" management thinking. Time and again, authors of best-selling business books, their publishers and the media would have us believe that the holy grail of strategy – *the strategy theory to put all previous ones to rest* – has finally been found. And indeed, a number of useful advances in strategic thinking have been made over the years. The fundamental problems facing managers today, however, are related to putting that strategy to work in the field of practice.

Yet, even strategy scholars are still grappling with the notion of strategy. As a concept, strategy still suffers from lack of precision in its definition. A number of significant gaps in the strategic management literature have left the discipline with a high degree of ambiguity, despite its popularity as a scholarly field of study. Rondo-Pupo and Guerras-Martin[1] in their recent study suggest the following reasons for this:

1. A paucity of knowledge of the evolution of the strategy concept in the field of strategic management;
2. A lack of consensus amongst scholars leading to significant diversity and ambiguity in definitions of the strategy concept;
3. Ambiguity in terms of the constituent elements of the strategy concept;
4. A lack of analysis and understanding regarding the structural evolution of the strategy concept; and
5. A lack of sufficient evidence supporting the understanding of the evolution of the strategy concept, and its influence on the field of strategic management.

Opposing views, on the other hand, have argued for the need to keep an element of conceptual diversity regarding the definition of the strategy concept; scholars, including Mintzberg[2] have argued that: " . . . *the field of strategic management cannot afford to rely on a single definition of strategy . . . explicit recognition of multiple definitions can help practitioners and researchers alike to maneuver through this difficult field . . .* ".

And so, the debate continues.

What then is "Strategy"?

In view of the proliferation of management publishing on the topic, it would seem reasonable to assume that we might at least begin with a clear and consistent definition of the notion of *strategy*. As has been argued in the previous section, however, this is not the case. Strategy has been defined in many different ways and it is still evolving as a concept. Early definitions of business strategy strongly imply deliberate planning and action, such as Chandler's[3] classic definition:

> The determination of the basic long-term goals and objectives of an enterprise, and the adoption of courses of action and the allocation of resources necessary for carrying out these goals.

Rondo-Pupo and Guerras-Martin[1] recently proposed the following definition of the strategy concept:

> . . . the dynamics of the firm's relation with its environment for which the necessary actions are taken to achieve its goals and/or to increase performance by means of the rational use of resources.

This definition, while an improvement on earlier definitions, still lacks clarity regarding the *purpose* of the goals in question. Invariably, these revolve around the ability, disposition and capacity of the firm to create and deliver *value* of some sort and format to its relevant stakeholders. The rational use of the firm's resources in response to opportunities and/or threats in its environment is no end in itself; clearly, the purpose of any activity on the part of the firm is to fulfill its obligations to its stakeholders through the creation and delivery of value. The form of that value created and delivered may range from explicit, readily measurable expressions of value to highly intangible, and difficult to measure forms of value. Indeed, the latter form of value is becoming increasingly important;

many value offerings today encompass both tangible and intangible components. As a case in point, consider a visit to Starbucks: no doubt the actual cup of coffee served over the counter has attributes of "measurable" value. However, Starbucks CEO Howard Schultz would view the "experience" associated with that visit to Starbucks – the complex amalgamation encompassing numerous tangible and intangible attributes of value delivery associated with the Starbucks visit such as the friendliness of the *barista* preparing and serving the coffee, the transaction over the counter, the ambience of the store setting, the cleanliness of the tables and chairs, in addition to the cup of coffee – to be the more important measure of the value delivered by Starbucks.

Consensus today appears to be forming around definitions of strategy that allow for the fact that strategy has both deliberate as well as unintended elements; that it is often only recognizable as such in retrospect. In this manner, Mintzberg[4] suggests thinking of strategy as a stream of actions, the meaning of which often becomes apparent only after their occurrence. Mintzberg also argues for thinking about strategy as a pretext for action positioned somewhere along a continuum that runs from purely deliberate to purely emergent, though in practice neither extreme is ever really encountered despite claims in the management literature suggesting otherwise.

So, rather than trying to nail down an exact definition of what strategy *is*, it is perhaps more evocative to reflect on what strategy is *about*.

From its earliest military origins, strategy has always been about gaining the competitive edge. We look back on several thousands of years of military history in which strategy has, in essence, always been about *winning*.

In a modern business context *winning* involves setting the right direction for an organization through periods of change and

Box 1.1 Lord Horatio Nelson: Strategy Lessons from Trafalgar

In the face of increasing complexity and ambiguity in their business environments companies are finding less space than ever for experimentation with their strategy. Competitive advantage, when gained, is often transient at best. However, while competitive contexts may be complex, the firm's approach to strategy needn't be. "Good" strategy needn't be the exception it mostly is; but it does demand both creativity and courage. We can derive lessons on what constitutes "good" strategy from Lord Horatio Nelson's winning naval engagement at Trafalgar in the autumn of 1805. At the time, England's sovereignty was under threat. Napoleon had conquered large parts of Europe and the invasion of England was next on his agenda. Napoleon's great hurdle was wresting control of the sea away from England in order to cross the Channel. Both sides met in a stand-off near the south west coast of Spain.

The French/Spanish combined fleet had 33 ships and the English 27. Lord Horatio Nelson commanded the outnumbered English fleet in that fateful naval confrontation just off the southwest coast of Spain at a point called Cape Trafalgar. Conventional battle strategy of the day dictated that opposing fleets stay in line firing broadsides at each other but Lord Horatio Nelson had another idea. Instead of lining up his ships broadside, he broke the English fleet into two columns and drove these perpendicularly into the French/Spanish fleet. The accompanying element of surprise and the superior ability of the English were asymmetries Nelson was banking on.

Nelson's gamble was that the less-trained French/Spanish gunners would not be able to compensate for the heavy swell that day. The outcome of the Battle of Trafalgar is well known: the French/Spanish lost 22 ships; the English lost none though Nelson himself was mortally wounded. Nelson's courageous strategy was that, although outnumbered, he risked his lead ships in an unexpected manoeuvre in order to break the coherence of the enemy ships. As this case nicely illustrates, good strategy is often deceptively simple; it revolves around the three key elements:

1. Grasping a few critical issues in the situation; this demands astute sense making, analysis and thereby, identification of potential asymmetries to be exploited.
2. Identifying appropriate pivot points through which these asymmetries can multiply the effectiveness of effort.
3. Focusing and concentrating coherent and cohesive action and resources to exploit the advantage offered through the asymmetries.

In practice, contexts and situations vary; they are complex and ambiguous. Nonetheless, the three basic elements of strategy reconstructed from the Nelson example do generally apply. In fact, the three elements constitute the basic three stages of the strategy process: (1) strategy analysis, (2) strategy option formation and (3) strategy execution or implementation.

securing its competitive well-being over time. By extension, a central research question that has emerged alongside the notion of *strategy as winning* is: "Why do some organizations persistently outperform others?"[5] Performance is assessed in terms of the value created and delivered to relevant stakeholders. An organization's competitive well-being rests on the organization's ability to *differentiate* itself – that is, being *different* – from its competitors. This was the basis of Nelson's victory; it is also the case in modern business strategy. In business strategy, firms must differentiate themselves on their ability to create and deliver a superior *value offering* to their stakeholders.

Box 1.2 The "Building Blocks" of Competitive Strategy

Strategy is inherently complex. Yet, we can identify simple components of a good strategy as we have seen earlier in this chapter. The essence of a sound strategy is captured by the following relatively few and deceptively simple questions; these comprise the basic building blocks of strategy:

1. What is the competitive economic environment in which we are competing? What are the key drivers? How are these changing?
2. What is our internal basis of competitiveness? On the basis of which resources, capabilities and practices are we competing? How do these provide us with an advantage relative to competitors? How is our competitive basis changing?
3. Who are our customers (and, in a broader sense, key stakeholders) today? Who will they be tomorrow? What do they/will they "need" and demand?
4. How do we align and orchestrate our organization's resources and capabilities to deliver uniquely superior value in response to our customers' needs; in other words, how do we "get our organizational act together"?
5. Given our understanding of the external context, our internal basis of competitiveness, and ability to create and deliver a uniquely superior value offering in response to customers' needs, what is our window of opportunity for creating unique value – our *unique competing space*? How is it changing?

When considered individually, the five building blocks appear to be relatively straightforward. In practice, the complex nature of strategy is reflected by the fact that these questions are often inextricably linked in real business contexts.

From this perspective, strategy appears to be rather straightforward: simply find responses to the set of basic questions outlined in Box 1.2 and the firm's strategy falls neatly into place. Why then are managers still struggling with strategy? There appear to be several plausible reasons for this. And, as is often the case in complex contexts, these are not entirely unrelated.

First, strategy is not *only* about rational analysis. Recent decades that have seen strategy evolve through a number of schools of thinking have ultimately put to rest the perception that strategy is simply an analytical problem to be solved with left-brain dexterity. Many of the approaches to "strategy" in the past have been shown not to have had much to do with strategy at all. In their place we find a growing number of diametrically opposed perspectives that underscore the paradoxical nature of strategy. Moreover, in messy, real-time strategy making there is no single "right" response. This insight has encouraged the search for insight "beyond the numbers" in strategy making. It has also given rise to a more comprehensive understanding of the roles and the importance of knowledge, intuition and human involvement in strategy. If nothing else, we have come to realize that strategic responses, no matter how seemingly appropriate, always remain shrouded in uncertainty to some extent. This residual uncertainty is introduced by complex environmental factors and the irrationality of human behavior.

Second, strategy is ultimately a practice discipline – as much as management is intrinsically a practice discipline. Many strategy scholars appear to neglect this. Strategy may start out as a paper exercise, but its ultimate test of validity occurs in the practice field. Practice fields are beset by complexity and ambiguity. In the practice field, we find an additional factor that often stands in the way of good strategy: many managers prefer *acting* (indeed, this is often a criterion for promotion) over *thinking*. In many corporate environments it is better to be seen doing something – *anything*, really – rather than to fall under the suspicion of inactivity (see Box 1.3 "A bias for action?"). Mintzberg[6] argues that managers often simply do not have or take the time to think. He points to studies showing that managers dislike reflective activities, and are strongly oriented to action. One particular study of British middle and top managers indicates that they worked without interruption for a half hour or more only about once every two days. Levy[7] points out, though, that deep reflection cannot be hurried and that insights cannot be forced; that both generally require substantial investments of time and sustained attention.

BOX 1.3 A BIAS FOR ACTION?

Topping the list of their "eight basic principles to stay on top of the heap", in the bestselling book entitled *In Search of Excellence*[8] by authors Peters and Waterman, we find "A bias for action: a preference for doing something – anything – rather than sending a question through cycles and cycles of analysis . . . ". Well, that advice appears to have resonated well with Percy Barnevik, former CEO of ABB. Barnevik believed in taking decisive action. He is said to have argued that: "1. To take action (and stick one's neck out) and do the right things is obviously the best behavior; 2. To take action and do the wrong things is next best (within reason and a limited number of times); 3. Not to take action (and lose opportunities) is the only unacceptable behavior." Barnevik elaborated in an interview with the *Financial Times*, asserting that "if you do 50 things, it is enough if 35 go in the right direction; . . . the only thing we cannot accept is people who do nothing".[9] This ethos involving action, initiative and risk-taking characterized ABB's culture and was often cited as a prime reason for its mercurial ascent in the 1990s. However, it was also at the root of a near-fatal business decision made in that same period. One of the companies acquired by ABB on its global acquisition spree was

> Combustion Engineering, a Stamford, Connecticut-based reactor vessel manufacturer. ABB acquired the firm in 1989; unfortunately, though, its due diligence failed to flag Combustion Engineering's history of using asbestos in its reactor linings. The resulting messy asbestos litigation almost nudged ABB over the brink of bankruptcy in the early 2000s. ABB was able to resolve the asbestos claims in a $1.43 billion settlement agreement only in 2006.[10]

Third, many managers are deeply uncomfortable with having to make strategic decisions under circumstances of incomplete information. There is still a persistent attitude in management circles that decisions need to be backed up with numbers – any numbers, even if these are often largely meaningless and effectively irrelevant to the issue in question. Business environments are complex and ambiguous, invariably non-quantifiable and continually changing. Therefore, only in a relatively few cases are numbers of even marginal significance available. Causality is all too often not apparent and the available information is therefore incomplete and asymmetric. Seldom does the "bigger picture" present itself in a cohesive manner. Yet, despite the lack of factual data, important strategic decisions often cannot wait. Business leaders must make decisions even in the face of inherent uncertainty and risk. That, after all, is their managerial task.

The list of circumstances and factors contributing to the strategy dilemma faced by managers today is long. Hence, we will only mention a final one for the sake of this argument: increasingly dynamic business environments are forcing managers to make decisions ever more quickly and on the run. This throws up a number of dilemmas: how can high-quality decisions be made quickly when critical information is incomplete or missing entirely, analysis is limited to a minimum, and debate and discourse – both necessary elements of good decision making – are suppressed in view of time constraints?

Given these circumstances, how should managers approach strategy in practice? This is the question we are seeking to address. We propose approaching strategy from the strategic thinking angle. The strategic thinking approach developed in this book is theoretically and conceptually rigorous while allowing for a range of possible strategy outcomes. In this respect it addresses the rapidly changing and complex reality managers experience in practice. It is about strategy *in practice* – the way it should be approached under circumstances of uncertainty and unpredictability.

Ultimately, strategy in practice is about achieving the right balance between *relevance* and *rigor* with respect to strategic thinking. *Relevance*, in as far as strategic thinking generates insights of strategic relevance and potential impact; *rigor* through proper grounding in current strategy theory. The approach to strategy taken in this book is largely consistent with the "strategy as process perspective" – yet without any presumption that strategy can or should be approached in a mechanistic way.

Indeed, the strategy process needs to capture and take into consideration all that is available to the manager – the "soft" insights coupled with collective experience that informs intuition from throughout the organization as well as any relevant "hard" data from analysis of the organization's external competitive context. Strategy making then involves synthesizing the collective learning through appropriate techniques of sense making and deriving from these insights suitable strategic options. To that end, strategic thinking is a complex process that, in Mintzberg's words, " . . . involves the most sophisticated, subtle, and at times, subconscious elements of human thinking".[11]

STRATEGY IN PRACTICE: POINTS FOR REFLECTION

- What are the tensions and dilemmas that typically surface when your organization engages in strategy?

- How are uncertainty, ambiguity and complexity dealt with in your organization?
- How much of the strategic insight in your organization is based on rational analysis (i.e. how much of it is largely numbers-driven); how much is based on intuition and "soft" information?
- What role does *strategic thinking* play in your organization's strategy process?

Where Does this Leave "Strategic Planning"?

It has been argued that *strategic planning* has little if anything to do with strategy at all. When it arrived on the scene in the 1960s, it was embraced by business leaders as *the* way to "make strategy". At the height of its popularity in the 1970s, corporations employed legions of strategic planners. Since then the realization has hit home that strategic planning really was little more than a controlling exercise that served the purpose of streamlining the rollout of strategies that were already in place. In essence it was about strategy programming and often stood in the way of strategic thinking.[12]

More than that, though, strategic planning represented a managerial mindset that sought the "one right answer" through purely rational analysis based on hard data. Managers seeking comfort in numbers recognized in it a way to mechanistically break a strategic objective down into manageable steps. The probability of the predictable was thought to be thereby maximized, the realization of desirable objectives assured.

Understandably, few business leaders today would be prepared to admit to traditional strategic planning. This doesn't mean, however, that strategic thinking has taken its place. Strategic thinking is not, and has never been, a core managerial capability in companies.[13] In many firms the strategic planning function has been replaced by *corporate development and planning*. These functions, however, are no substitute for good strategic thinking in these organizations.

BOX 1.4 ROBERT MCNAMARA: THE "ENLIGHTENED RATIONALIST"

Few senior managers have epitomized strategic planning more than the late Robert McNamara (1916–2009), one of the ten "Whiz Kids" Ford Motor Company hired in 1946 to shake up its business. McNamara was later plucked from Ford by John F. Kennedy to be US Secretary of Defense. A former Harvard economics professor, he loved numbers. Things that could be counted, McNamara maintained, ought to be counted. He was an iconic planning manager who could use facts, numbers and analyses to solve any problem, even to wage wars in far-off Vietnam. There were the four McNamara steps to running an organization: the first, stating an objective; second, working out how to get there; third, costing out everything; and lastly, systematically monitoring progress against plan. The Vietnam War became widely known as "McNamara's War". McNamara didn't know anything about Vietnam – nor did those around him. But then, the American attitude in that era was that one didn't have to know the culture or history of a place in order to engage in successful warfare in the respective theatre. What was needed was the right data, a proper analysis of the information and an application of military superiority to win the war. McNamara spearheaded the Pentagon's effort in Vietnam until 1968. McNamara applied all the right metrics – bombing missions flown, targets hit, captives taken, weapons seized, the enemy's body-count. Another metric, the American troops' own body-count, at some point began informing him with equal certainty that America was losing the war. Initially this baffled

McNamara. Things began unraveling seriously in 1965. Ordered to win the war, McNamara stepped up his statistical war of attrition by approving ever more troop increases. On the home front, resistance to the war grew. At the height of the conflict he was denounced as a baby-burner; his own son joined in the protest marches against him. As he later admitted in his penitent memoirs, he had learned the hard way that he had not understood the variables of war itself – most important of which was that numbers capture neither the human condition nor human activity. As McNamara came to realize, hard quantitative data can have a decidedly soft and qualitative underbelly. In the case of the Vietnam War, human factors played a decisive role – the enemy Vietcong made every single person count. Of the 11 lessons to be learned from McNamara's war in Vietnam, regrettably, this and most of the others occurred to him too late to be of much help.

Sources: 1. *The Economist*, Obituary on Robert McNamara (11 July 2009); 2.*TIME (Europe)*, L.H. Gelb: Remembrance – Robert McNamara (20 July 2009).

Insight-driven Strategy

Insight plays a key role in the strategic thinking process. While we explore the notion of insight in greater detail in Chapter 3, suffice it to say here that insight formation involves a complex combination of analysis and intuition – and that not all insight is equally relevant or useful to strategic thinking. The key to good strategic thinking lies in knowing what insight to seek and pursue. Collis and Montgomery[14] argue that two potentially powerful insights relate to the organization's capabilities and the competition it faces. These delineate the opportunity for creating unique value, which in turn forms the basis of competitive differentiation.

Strategic insight is an outcome of the strategic thinking process; hence the emphasis in this book on an *insight-driven* approach to strategy. Strategic thinking is the vehicle for delivering insight. It provides the systematic and structured approach that draws on *sense making* to bring into balance rational analysis and intuition, experienced-derived judgment and knowledge. Leonard and Swap[15] refer to the collective outcome of these components as "deep smarts". Strategic insights serve a number of purposes. They are outcomes of sense making at individual stages of the strategic thinking process. However, they also help to guide and align the thinking process through its various stages. Ultimately, individual strategic insights, when collated like pieces of a puzzle, contribute to the emergence of a reconstructed "bigger picture" of the firm's competitive landscape. Inevitably, this picture is never complete. However, if properly executed, the strategic thinking process ensures that the pattern which emerges is sufficient to identify potentially suitable options for strategic action. To that end, strategic insights collectively contribute to and enable the formation of potentially suitable strategic options in the emerging competitive context. Strategy formation is a dynamic process that presents the strategist with a range of options, of which one represents the most suitable option. Seldom, however, does a single "right" strategic response emerge as an outcome of this activity. In practice, the selection of a strategic option involves some degree of compromise. Insight supports the process whereby options are evaluated and ultimately selected.

Real competitive environments are highly complex and messy. This presents limits to the degree to which strategy making can be formalized. We need to allow for circumstances under which strategies emerge inadvertently, without deliberate intention on the part of the organization's management. The premise of this book is that while real strategy is not programmable as such, it does not mean that our approach to strategy needs to be haphazard. The purpose of this book is to guide the reader through the thinking process that results in good strategy making in a real-time context.

> ## STRATEGY IN PRACTICE: INSIGHT-DRIVEN STRATEGY VERSUS STRATEGIC PLANNING
>
> - Today's fast-paced, continually changing competitive environment leaves little room for the strategic planning approaches practiced in many companies throughout the 1970s and 1980s; few companies today enjoy environments that allow any meaningful planning by numbers in timeframes of five and more years into the future.
> - Insight-driven strategy enables a very different approach; while offering a systematic and structured strategic thinking framework, it draws on multiple inputs and variable timeframes; it balances the hard numbers (where available) with the "soft" indicators emerging from complex contexts.
> - The key to implementing an insight-driven approach to strategy begins with a mindset that is prepared to challenge assumptions and that is comfortable with non-quantifiable measures and inputs.
> - Paraphrasing Kevin Kelly,[16] insight-driven strategy "seeks not so much to perfect the known, rather to imperfectly seize the unknown"; it is congruent with an organizational culture that embraces experimentation and learning.
> - What is your organization's mindset? One that is more in tune with strategic planning or one that is amenable to insight-driven strategy?

"Strategy in Practice" or "Strategy as Practice"?

This book is about "strategy *in* practice". It aims to provide guidance to the management practitioner engaging with strategy in the practice field. Hence, it is about how strategy should be approached *in practice*. How is the focus on strategy practice pursued in this book different from the school of thought that has emerged in recent years known as "strategy *as* practice"? To the extent that the latter focuses on bringing the *thinking* element back into strategy,[17,18] the approach developed in this book is largely consistent with the underlying conceptual thrust of the "strategy as practice" school. However, this book neither purports nor aspires to contribute to the institutionalization of any particular school of strategy, including the "strategy as practice" approach (which, incidentally, has been critiqued for adopting an unclear and contradictory definition of "strategy practice"[19]). The purpose of this book is first and foremost to provide the strategy practitioner with the appropriate managerial wherewithal for strategic thinking, not to contribute to the cause of any particular school of strategy.

Summary and Structuring of the Book

This chapter began with a review of the current dilemma most business leaders face when confronted with strategy and strategy making, despite the proliferation of strategy theory in recent years. Given the ongoing discourse on what strategy *is*, it is probably more meaningful to focus on what strategy is *about*. It is about winning; about achieving superior performance relative to competitors in creating and delivering a superior value offering. Ultimately, however, strategy is a *practice discipline*. Indeed, many of the difficulties experienced by managers in dealing with strategy relate to the sheer complexity, ambiguity and messiness of management practice in the competitive environments of organizations. This requires a strategic thinking process that draws on a balanced combination of systematic analysis and intuition leading to insights relevant to strategy making, hence the centrality of the theme *insight-driven* strategy.

The following chapters of this book (shown schematically in Figure 1.1) lead through the insight-driven strategic thinking

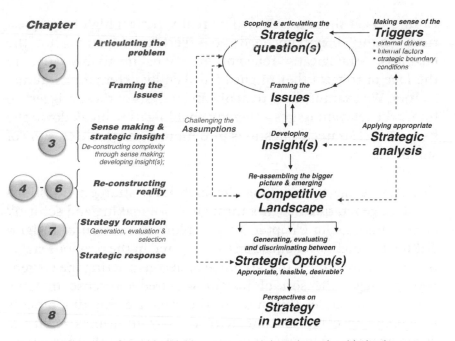

Figure 1.1 Strategic thinking process and roadmap for this book

process. We begin with the articulation of appropriate strategic questions in Chapter 2. Managers and their teams are often at a loss where to begin with strategy. In Chapter 2 we focus particular attention on the "fuzzy front end" of the strategy process. A lot is at stake at this stage; setting off in the wrong direction by only a few degrees ultimately leads to large deviations and failure down the road. Strategy necessarily begins with knowing where to concentrate the thinking effort. While there may be many problems facing a company, getting to the core of the strategic problem and framing those questions that will really make the difference is the key to getting started. Presumably there are many seemingly important questions of strategic relevance that demand to be addressed by a business leader – yet, arguably, the ones that at any point in time really make a disproportionate difference to the company's competitive positioning are relatively few in number.

Failure to get those relatively few really critical high-level questions "right" inevitably leads to severe consequences for the business. Strategically relevant questions invariably arise in the face of triggers that might be driven by external or internal factors. We examine how to apply an analysis of these triggers to frame the relevant issues – thereby enabling us to break down the higher-level strategic questions into more manageable clusters of sub-questions.

The next stage to resolving the high-level strategic questions involves generating insights through sense making and scrutiny of assumptions. In Chapter 3 we explore the notion of insight. Taking the high-level questions articulated in the previous stage, issues that are framed in the course of deconstructing the current reality trigger the sort of insight required for sense making. Chapter 3 describes this stage of the strategic thinking process in which the complex context of the organization's reality is deconstructed through judicious application of appropriate frameworks and tools of strategic analysis. Intuition plays an important guiding role at this stage as well. Intuition guides the selection and piecing together of the insights that emerge from the sense making. It is essential for the contextualization of the situation under investigation. The bits and pieces of insight that emerge from this sense making exercise as well as the intuition that has been drawn on for this stage are then subjected to reality checks through scrutiny and challenging of assumptions.

Chapters 4 through 6 are devoted to the subject of strategic analysis. In Chapter 4 we derive the general context for strategic analysis. We examine how analysis is used to generate insights required for strategic sense making. This is followed by an introduction to *high-level* analysis and frameworks of strategic analysis in Chapter 5. In Chapter 6 we introduce the *supporting levels* of strategic analysis and derive their purpose and application in the context of strategic sense making. A basic premise of this book is that a few good frameworks applied appropriately to support strategic thinking can yield a disproportionate amount of insight. It is important to know which frameworks to use and how to use them. In Chapter 6 we review some of the more useful frameworks, their application and their limitations. In this chapter we also explore how the insights generated during the sense making stage are subsequently assembled – not unlike pieces of a puzzle in the reconstruction of a bigger picture that represents the competitive landscape of the organization in question, albeit an incomplete one. Intuition again plays an important role during this stage. Research on intuition suggests that its usefulness at this stage derives from insight related to reflected experience[20] – experience in knowing what to look for, where to look and how to integrate the new insights into an existing pattern of understanding. Intuition enables the experienced strategist to perceive patterns where many might not. This is often all there is to go on for decision making – management reality is riddled with incomplete pictures that beg nonetheless to be appropriately interpreted and to be made sense of.

Up to this point the focus has been on strategic thinking and sense making. Strategic thinking and sense making, if properly executed, have enabled us to identify a bigger picture, which even if incomplete, nonetheless reflects the relevant attributes of the firm's competitive landscape. We might well ask at this stage: so, what now? In Chapter 7 we explore how we use the outcome of strategic thinking and sense making to create appropriate strategic options. This stage focuses on the derivation of strategic options; on the formation of suitable strategy. Strategy formation is highly dependent on the specific circumstances (maturity, size, configuration and other factors) of a firm. We draw on an approach proposed by Mintzberg (2009)[21] that categorizes firms' strategy making mechanisms according to four basic configurations; these reflect degree of maturity and dynamics of the competitive environment. We explore the implications of strategy formation in practice.

Once formed, options must be evaluated and narrowed down to one or possibly two that represent the most appropriate choice under the given circumstances. We close Chapter 7 with a review of some systematic approaches to evaluating and selecting suitable strategic options.

In Chapter 8, the final chapter of the book, we close with reflections on strategic thinking and insight-driven strategy from various practice field perspectives. We explore why organizational configurations show variations in their predisposition for strategy making. We derive implications for the organization by exploring both the scope and limitations of strategic thinking set against constraints imposed by the reality of firms' competitive context and dynamics. In this way, the book ends with a reality check and some recommendations for enhancing the impact of strategic thinking.

The Appendix section of this book presents some practical applications of the concepts and approaches introduced and discussed throughout the book. These exercises provide a structured approach for putting these into practice.

It is only appropriate that we review some final caveats and pointers before delving into the strategic thinking framework which is examined in the subsequent chapters – the final boxed insert below summarizes these:

STRATEGY IN PRACTICE: SOME PRACTICAL POINTERS ON THE STRATEGIC THINKING FRAMEWORK

- The strategic thinking framework mapped in Figure 1.1 is not intended to be used mechanistically. Management reality is intrinsically complex and riddled with ambiguity. Any approach to strategy making must reflect this reality. Therefore, the strategic thinking process proposed in this book is primarily to guide and challenge the strategy practitioner's thinking and reasoning process from the articulation of compelling strategic questions through to their appropriate resolution.

- Although the structure of the framework would suggest a series of "top-down" activities, the strategic thinking process is, in fact, highly iterative and features multiple feedback loops throughout.
- There is no single "right answer"; there is no "one-size-fits-all" in strategy. Management situations are highly contextual. A response that addresses the circumstances of the complex contexts in question often calls for compromise between possible solution approaches. Therefore, the outcome of the strategic thinking process should be viewed in terms of strategic options that range from "suitable" to those that are clearly "less than appropriate". The framework enables the strategy practitioner to develop substantive arguments in support of the most suitable strategy option.
- The framework relegates strategic tools of analysis to where they belong – in a supportive role, to be drawn on very selectively to develop relevant insight where required. Managers often find themselves entangled in the dense undergrowth of strategy frameworks, thereby losing sight of the wood for the undergrowth. There is no end to the sophistication of strategy tools nowadays.
- Used appropriately, however, even simple frameworks such as the *SWOT* (strengths, weaknesses, opportunities, threats) framework can deliver useful pieces of the puzzle to be constructed. We will see in Chapter 6 how some relatively simple models can be integrated into more comprehensive, integrated frameworks that in turn can deliver powerful insights.

Notes

1. Rondo-Pupo, G.A. and Guerras-Martin, L.A. (2012) Dynamics of the Evolution of the Strategy Concept 1962–2008: A Co-Word Analysis, *Strategic Management Journal*, 33, pp. 162–188.

2. Mintzberg, H. (1995) Five Ps for Strategy, in Mintzberg, H., Quinn, J.B. and Ghoshal, S. (eds) *The Strategy Process, European Edition*, London: Prentice Hall, pp. 13–21.
3. Chandler, A.D. (1962) *Strategy and Structure*, Cambridge, MA: MIT Press.
4. Mintzberg, H. (2009) *Tracking Strategies – Toward a General Theory*, Oxford: Oxford University Press.
5. Barney, J.B. and Clark, D.N. (2007) *Resource-Based Theory*, Oxford: Oxford University Press.
6. Mintzberg, H. (1990) The Manager's Job: Folklore and Fact, *Harvard Business Review*, March–April.
7. Levy, D.M. (2008) Wanted: Time to Think, *MIT Sloan Management Review*, Fall, 21–24.
8. Peters, T.J. and Waterman Jr, R.H. (1982) *In Search of Excellence*, New York: Warner Books.
9. Rosenzweig, P. (2007) *The Halo Effect*, New York: Free Press.
10. *Boston Globe* (1st September 2006): ABB says Lummus Asbestos Claims Resolved (Reuters).
11. Mintzberg, H. (1994) The Fall and Rise of Strategic Planning, *Harvard Business Review*, January–February, pp. 107–114.
12. Mintzberg, H. (1995) (note 2 above).
13. Christensen, C.M. (1997) Making Strategy: Learning by Doing, *Harvard Business Review*, November–December.
14. Collis, D.J. and Montgomery, C.A. (2008) Competing on Resources, *Harvard Business Review*, July–August, pp. 140–150.
15. Leonard, D.L. and Swap, W. (2005) *Deep Smarts: Experience-Based Wisdom*, Boston: Harvard Business School Press.
16. Kelly, K. (1998) *New Rules for the New Economy*, New York: Viking.
17. Whittington, R. (2002) Practice Perspectives on Strategy: Unifying and Developing a Field, *Best Paper Proceedings*, Academy of Management, Denver.
18. Balogun, J.P., Jarzabkowski, P. and Seidl, D. (2007) Strategy as Practice Perspective, in Jenkins, M., Ambrosini, V. and Collier, N. (eds) *Advanced Strategic Management*, 2nd ed., Basingstoke: Palgrave Macmillan.
19. Carter, C.S., Clegg, R. and Kornberger, M. (2008) *A Very Short, Fairly Interesting and Reasonably Cheap Book About Studying Strategy*, London: Sage Publications Ltd.
20. Eisenhardt, K.M. (2008) Speed and Strategic Choice: How Managers Accelerate Decision Making, *California Management Review*, 50(2 Winter), pp. 102–116.
21. Mintzberg, H. (2009) (note 4 above).

CHAPTER 2

Articulating the Strategic Question

If only I had the right question . . . if only I had the right question; . . . the formulation of the problem is often more important than its solution.

—Albert Einstein

IN THIS CHAPTER, WE:

- establish and argue the case for the importance of articulating the "right" strategic questions;
- explore the potential origin of good strategic questions;
- examine how the right strategic questions are formulated;
- explore how questions are triggered and how these lead to issues that require framing and analysis;
- examine the importance of challenging assumptions and the prevailing industry logic.

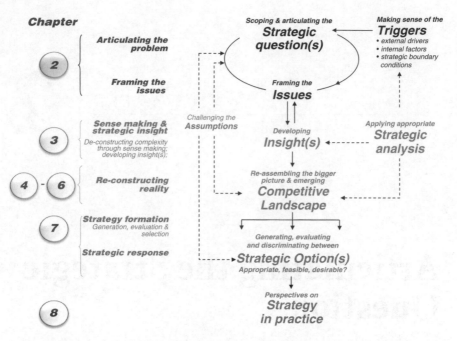

Figure 2.1 Strategic thinking and issues framing in the greater context of strategic thinking

What's in a question? A lot, potentially. The German theoretical physicist and philosopher Werner Heisenberg[1] argued that nature reveals itself to us by virtue of the questions we ask. Nature does not reveal itself by asking just any question; hence it is critical that appropriate questions are asked.

In this chapter we explore how strategic questions are formulated and their role in the strategic thinking process. Strategic questions represent the starting point of the strategic thinking process as indicated in Figure 2.1.

The importance of articulating the right questions for the physical sciences is easily extended to the social context: contexts relevant to the firm's competitive well-being also reveal themselves by our manner of questioning. Asking the "right" questions from the outset is therefore critical to any strategic thinking exercise. What are "right" strategic questions? We will explore this question

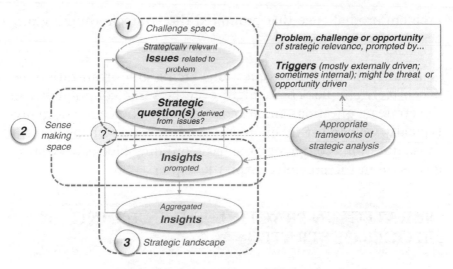

Figure 2.2 Strategic questions and issues framing

further in this chapter; suffice it to say that the "right" questions are those that address problems and issues that are of strategic relevance and importance to an organization (Figure 2.2). They might be strategically relevant in the near or long term. Good strategic questions address those relatively few high-level, high-priority issues facing the business that have the greatest potential for competitive impact. Failure to correctly identify questions of this caliber leads to strategic aimlessness at best, and business disaster at worst. Articulating the right strategic questions is the starting point for the strategic thinking process.

Just as important is the proper sequencing of the strategic thinking process once triggered, as suggested in Figure 2.2. The first important stage is the *challenge space* (labeled *"1"*) in which issues and questions are challenged as to their relevance. Once this has been established, the next stage comprises the *sense making space* (*"2"* in Figure 2.2). Strategic questions derived from the foregoing challenge space prompt *insights* to be generated through sense making, supported by strategic analysis. In the final *strategic landscape* space (*"3"*) insights are aggregated to form a reconstruction of the firm's strategic reality relevant to the problem or challenge that prompted the strategic thinking process in the first instance.

Generally, the high-level questions facing any organization are deceptively simple. There might even be some commonality of the strategic questions among competitors. There are not many; typically we can list them on one hand. A good starting point is those questions comprising the basic building blocks of strategy discussed in the previous chapter (Chapter 1; Box 1.2).

STRATEGY IN PRACTICE: THE BUILDING BLOCKS OF STRATEGY

Invariably, questions of strategic relevance address one or more of the building blocks of strategy introduced in the previous chapter:

- What is the competitive economic environment in which we are competing? What are the key drivers? How are these changing?
- What is our basis of competitiveness? On the basis of which resources, capabilities and practices are we competing? How do these provide us with an advantage relative to competitors? How is our competitive basis changing?
- Who are our customers (and, in a broader sense, key stakeholders) today? Who will they be tomorrow? What do they/ will they "need" and demand?
- How do we align and orchestrate our organization's resources and capabilities to deliver uniquely superior value in response to our customers' needs; in other words, how do we "get our organizational act together"?
- Given our understanding of the external context, our internal basis of competitiveness and ability to create and deliver a uniquely superior value offering in response to customers' needs, what is our window of opportunity for creating unique value – our *unique competing space*? How is it changing?

Of particular importance are those questions probing problems or challenges of strategic relevance to the organization. "Strategic" in this context refers to the fact that the question is relevant to the organization's ability to compete – its competitiveness. Inevitably, strategic questions arise when conditions affecting the organization's ability to compete change. Changes are most often triggered by factors external to the organization; at times, however, strategic questions arise when the organization's internal basis of competitiveness changes. Strategic questions, though, might also be triggered by a combination of both external and internal factors that have an impact on the enterprise's competitive position.

Inevitably, there are many problems and challenges facing an organization at any one point in time. Only relatively few, however, are of disproportionate importance – that is, of real strategic relevance. Arguably, therefore, the high-level task of a senior manager is a relatively simple one: it is to identify the two or three really top priority strategic problems (or possibly opportunities) facing the organization and to get on with the task of resolving (or exploiting) these. Failure on the part of the senior manager to get a handle on the few really important questions leads to strategic drift and loss of competitive focus. In management we talk about the "Pareto"[2] principle. Also known as the "80–20 rule", it suggests that 80% of the impact comes from 20% of the causes – for example, that 80% of an enterprise's profitability stems from 20% of its products. From a strategic perspective the Pareto principle would suggest focusing one's efforts on those few questions that really stand to make a difference. The real crux of this stage in the strategic thinking process, of course, lies in identifying those few really critical high-level strategic questions. This is not a trivial task.

Strategic Questions

Good strategic questions are triggered by problems or challenges that address the core purpose of an organization – its ability to create and deliver value to its stakeholders. Often, the problem centers on changes in the organization's competitive ability to do so. Perhaps a new competitor in the market is threatening the organization's competitive position. Possibly, the organization has lost its ability to compete in its markets due to neglect of its strategic resource base. Perhaps it has lost its sense of direction in terms of its shared sense of purpose and guiding values. All of these are challenges of a competitive nature. Problems and challenges, however, need not necessarily be negatively loaded. They might relate to an emerging opportunity in the market that calls for clarification and possibly action. Problems, in order to merit our attention, must be *strategically relevant*, meaning they must fall into the category of the "important few" that have a potentially high business impact. These are the ones that have an important long-term positive impact on the competitive position of the organization in question. Failure to achieve resolution will have a potentially significant negative impact on the competitive well-being of the firm in question.

Problems and challenges have owners. We call them *stakeholders*. These are the people or institutions that stand to gain (or lose) most by a problem's successful (or failed) resolution. Stakeholders' needs, power and legitimacy of claim relative to the problem vary. Hence we differentiate between stakeholders with high legitimacy and a strong position to influence, and those with marginal legitimacy and less power to influence the outcome of the problem's resolution. The first group is important; they are the *key stakeholders*.

Strategically relevant problems invariably arise as a result of *changes* in the firm's competitive context. Broadly categorized, these might lie in any of the three areas listed in the box below.

STRATEGY IN PRACTICE: GETTING THE HIGH-LEVEL STRATEGIC QUESTIONS "RIGHT"

How does one get the strategic questions "right"? While there are no hard and fast rules for articulating the right high-level strategic questions, these typically emerge from diligent and continual effort in the following three activity clusters:

1. *Continual monitoring of the external environment* for developments that might lead to changes in the competitive playing field. Strategic questions, when they arise, are inevitably triggered by changing conditions. Most often these will be externally driven. A simple *PESTEL* (political, economic, societal, technological, environmental and legal) factor scan is always a good starting point. Changing conditions of competition prompt strategic questions of the type: "What has changed, and why?"

2. *Scrutinizing the changing conditions for their strategic (competitive) relevance.* Changes in the competitive environment may have implications for the organization's ability to compete. Multiple changes (change on various fronts), which are becoming ever more the rule, may have a coupled and synergetic overall impact on the organization's competitive position. Strategic questions prompted by scrutiny of change are of the type: "What are the implications of the changes for the organization, and why so?"

3. *Probing for appropriate responses on the part of the organization to the changing competitive condition.* Changing conditions that have strategic relevance for the organization demand appropriate response. While external factors prompting the changing conditions of competition generally cannot be influenced, these will prompt high-level strategic questions within the organization of the type: "What should the organization be doing; what can it do in response to the changing conditions?"

Triggers

Changes in the Organization's External Competitive Environment

Strategic questions may be triggered by problems arising as a result of change in the firm's *external environment*. Change of this type might be driven by any number, or even combinations, of external factors such as sociopolitical change, technological advances, increasing competition through new competitors, demographic changes in the firm's customer base and markets, and other external macroeconomic drivers. As a rule, external factors such as these lie beyond the control of any individual firm. There is little any individual firm can do to influence these external factors. Not all drivers will be equally important; not all will have the same potential impact on the organization's competitive position. However, organizations need to understand the relevant drivers in their external environment. More than that, they need to understand the dynamics of the relevant drivers. Not all will be changing at the same rate; some will be changing more than others. Organizations need to understand and track the dynamics of those external drivers with the greatest potential competitive impact.

Changes in Internal Competing Factors

Strategic questions might also arise as a result of strategically relevant problems that have their source within the organization. These are factors which the organization, as a rule, *can* influence. Such problems might be the result of negligence or failure on the part of the firm to engage in appropriate and timely activities. This might include, for example, failure on the part of the organization to develop strategic resources in response to changing market demands; or when an organization neglects to nurture an organizational culture that supports a strategically critical capability, such as innovation. The problem may have multiple dimensions, all of which are internal to the organization. In the case of an inferior innovation capability these might include a missing managerial systems infrastructure, a culture that punishes trying and failing, or a lack of cutting edge knowledge. The problem might manifest itself in multiple ways as well – continual failure to bring new products to market might be one such expression that leads to follow-on problems, one of which might be the inability to subsequently attract the best talent as a result of a tarnished reputation in the market place.

Most often strategic questions are not well articulated. Many fail to address the essence of the organization's current dilemma altogether. Strategic questions that succeed in focusing the thinking on matters central to the organization's core purpose of creating and delivering a uniquely superior value offering usually present a good starting point.

Let's explore the articulation of good strategic questions more deeply with the help of a concrete example: Swiss coffee maker *Nespresso*'s current strategic situation in view of expiring patents on its highly successful single-serve coffee pod concept.

Box 2.1 Nespresso – What Next?

Nespresso, one of those companies that have succeeded in generating eye-wateringly lucrative returns to its investors, is currently at a critical crossroads. In the quarter century since its (admittedly, shaky early) launch the company has managed to protect its near-monopoly position with an array of patents – in total about 1,700 – that cover the individual coffee capsules, their composition, and the delivery system consisting of machines that inject steam and water into a hermetically-sealed aluminum capsule containing ground coffee. The result is a high-quality cup of *espresso* featuring a perfect *crema* (foam), consistently so. The Nestlé subsidiary reportedly achieved sales of CHF 3.5 billion (GBP 2.3 billion) of its coffee capsules and still commands healthy double-digit (" . . . *around 20 percent*") sales growth. Margins are estimated to be in excess of 25 percent. The real margins, however, according to Jean-Paul Gaillard, the former *Nestlé* manager who ran *Nespresso* for a decade before leaving the company to return as a main competitor, are in the capsulized coffee pods, for which consumers pay about five times the price of what they would normally pay for regular roasted coffee.

However, a number of threatening clouds are appearing on *Nespresso*'s horizon. This is particularly the case in austerity-hit Europe, where fierce competition appears to remain largely unaffected by the prevailing economic crisis in the fast-growing premium single-cup coffee market. No doubt, *Nespresso*'s success, supported by astute market positioning of its coffee pod as "the closest thing to a luxury brand within fast-moving consumer goods" and clever advertising featuring US actor George Clooney, has attracted considerable competition. Most recently, *Starbucks* announced its intentions to enter into this space. At the time of this writing, there are an estimated 50 mimicking systems in the market.

More worrying, however, is the fact that many of the 1,700 patents protecting the *Nespresso* system are set to expire this year (2012). *Nespresso* has not sat back idly; it has launched legal action against a number of new entrants, including Gaillard's *Ethical Coffee Company*, which has introduced a less-pricey bio-degradable coffee pod that is otherwise compatible with existing *Nespresso* machines. While loath to reveal any of its product plans, there is speculation that *Nespresso* is working on electronic identification technology that will enable future machines to recognize and function only with *Nespresso* branded coffee capsules.

Be that as it may, a lot is currently at stake for *Nespresso*. What it arguably fears most at this point is a credible alternative to its provocative advertising slogan: "*Nespresso, what else*"?

Sources: 1. Lucas, L. and Simonian, H. (2012) Rivals Eye Nestlé's Captive Market, *Financial Times* (10–11 March 2012); 2. Nespresso Plans a Third Factory to Make Capsules, *Financial Times* (4 May 2012); 3. Alderman, L. (2010) Nestlé Fights to Defend its Pods of Liquid Gold, *International Herald Tribune/New York Times Global Edition* (21–22 August 2012).

There are many questions *Nespresso* managers might be asking at this point in view of the challenges they are facing. While the questions will vary in respect of their priority, one can assume that only relatively few questions will carry the potential to make a disproportionately significant difference. These are the questions *Nespresso* managers will want to flag and address.

One such question, no doubt, might be a conceivably simple one: "What's changed?" Clearly many things have changed over the period of *Nespresso*'s double-digit growth over the past two decades or so. Getting a handle on what has changed is an important first step in any strategic sense making exercise. There have been significant changes in *Nespresso*'s external competitive environment, its internal ability to compete – perhaps even in its core purpose and paradigm – over the period in question. To be very clear, *Nespresso* managers would not be starting at a "point zero" when formulating the simple question regarding change in their competitive context. Nonetheless, they will need to gain clarity on this level before moving to any further questions that probe possible options. A proper framing of the relevant issues associated with the changes in *Nespresso*'s competitive context, both external and internal, is an appropriate launching point for this exercise.

Framing the Issues

Issue analyses involve a further refinement of high-level strategic questions. A high-level strategic question always consists of multiple components. These reflect the complexity of the problem requiring analysis. A framing of the issues helps us to segment a strategic question into its more manageable component parts. Clusters of issues that emerge from the framing exercise relate to the various triggers that have given rise to the strategic problem in the first place. Figure 2.3 suggests how this might be approached.

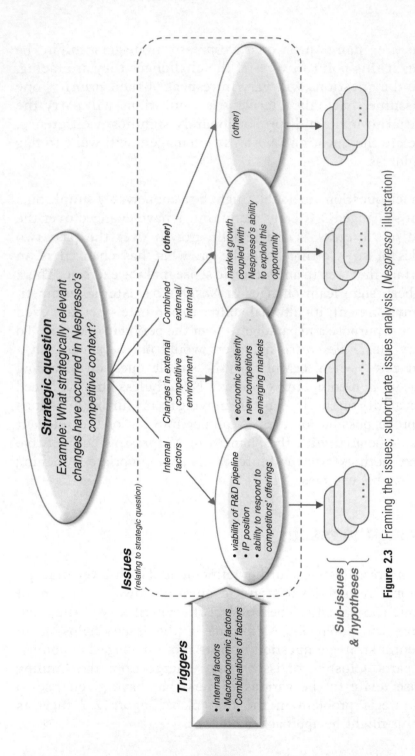

Figure 2.3 Framing the issues; subordinate issues analysis (*Nespresso illustration*)

Strategic question

Example: What strategically relevant changes have occurred in Nespresso's competitive context?

Issues
(relating to strategic question)

Internal factors

Changes in external competitive environment

Combined external/internal

(other)

(other)

• viability of R&D pipeline
• IP position
• ability to respond to competitors' offerings

• economic austerity
• new competitors
• emerging markets

• market growth coupled with Nespresso's ability to exploit this opportunity

(other)

Sub-issues & hypotheses

Triggers

• Internal factors
• Macroeconomic factors
• Combinations of factors

The strategic question is reviewed from the perspective of the various triggers. These might relate to internal factors, macro-economic trends, or combinations of external and internal factors. Relevant clusters of issues are identified for each of the triggers. This level of issues is then broken down even further into clusters of sub-issues, and so on.

Remaining with the *Nespresso* example, one way of framing issues around the simple high-level question: "What's changed?" would be to identify possible triggers or drivers of change that might have an impact on *Nespresso's* competitive position. The changes queried by the strategic question, broadly speaking, have been triggered by changing conditions in one, possibly two or even combinations of factors in the following categories: (1) changes in *Nespresso's* internal basis of competitiveness; (2) changes in its *external context.* Issues relating to *Nespresso's* internal factors might include the viability of its current R&D pipeline; possible ramifications of its legal action against competitors' product offerings. In the next category we would expect to find some impact of the current economic crisis; socio-economic factors may also have changed the profile of the typical *Nespresso* customer. Certainly, the nature of competition – increasing numbers of competitors with comparable product and service offerings – has changed in *Nespresso's* markets.

Issues can be further broken down into clusters of subordinate issues as shown in Figure 2.3; these, in turn, can be extended even further. The point at which the issues cascade terminates depends largely on the level at which a strategic response is required.

Assumptions, Hypotheses and Prevailing Logic

A hypothesis is a hunch, an educated guess or simply a proposition to be validated by further investigation. Hypotheses serve as guiding ideas and a first stage of forming insight on the questions flagged by the issues analysis. They are in fact tentative framing views that need to be challenged and ultimately validated, modified or even refuted outright. An assumption is a hypothesis that has become taken for granted. Assumptions reflect our deep beliefs and the paradigm we identify with. Schein (1992)[3] defines assumptions as being close to the core of an organization's culture. Their origin lies deep within the organization's substrata characterized by the unconscious and tacit frames that shape the organization's values and paradigm in the subconscious realm. Assumptions are therefore often difficult to discern.

However, assumptions do determine how we identify and define problems, much as they influence the way in which we derive solution approaches. The assumptions business leaders make when thinking about their competitive situation reflect the prevailing mindset within the organization. By extension, the assumptions shared across an industry reflect the prevailing *industry logic*. The prevailing mindset expresses itself in terms of the *business paradigm*. The business paradigm, in turn, is a coherent set of assumptions and perceptions that find expression in the business's practices, values and norms. An organization's business paradigm reflects its take on reality, where it perceives opportunities and threats in its market place.

Box 2.2 Fateful French Assumptions

The German invasion of France in May 1940 should not have been the pushover it ended up being. The French military was invincible. Their officer corps was battle-hardened from the Great War. French defenses included the impenetrable Maginot Line and the French military's intelligence gathering was superb – or so the French thought. In fact, not only the French but others at the time thought so as well. The German general staff is said to have plotted a coup against Hitler already in late 1939 because they thought his plan to attack France absolutely insane.

So, what went wrong? Military historian Ernest May[4] suggests that the French failed to challenge a number of very basic assumptions concerning their defenses and an impending German assault. Although the French were clearly aware of the German threat, particularly following the *Blitzkrieg* assault on Poland, they were prepared for every scenario except the one that actually took place. The French assumption was that since the Ardennes Forest was impassable to heavy tanks the Germans would attack France through Belgium. Consequently, this was where the French concentrated their defenses. Another unchallenged assumption of the French was that their forces were better trained and disciplined than the Polish forces, hence the French assumed the *Blitzkrieg* scenario to be irrelevant. A final assumption that proved fatal to the French was that the German high command would behave rationally and not attempt an assault through the Ardennes. In this respect the French reacted no differently than many organizations today: they were blinded by their almost religious faith that the past is a prologue to all futures.

In retrospect we know that events unfolded very differently: the Germans did the unexpected, the Ardennes turned out to be passable after all. The extraordinary success of the invasion of France was largely due to the efforts of the Generals Erich von Manstein and Heinz Guderian, who perfected and deployed the so-called "sickle-cut" (the metaphor is said to have originated with Churchill) offensive to outmaneuver French fortifications and reduce any potential impact the French military's superior numbers in men and material might have had.

The German *Blitzkrieg* strategy worked just as well in the West as it had in the East. Despite their smaller size German forces overwhelmed France within a matter of weeks. The Allies had simply not anticipated a disciplined and swift offensive by the Germans through the Ardennes Forest. In his treatise, May argues that the German general staff, moreover, correctly anticipated that the French high command would (a) dispatch most of the first-line forces to Belgium; (b) not recognize for several days that this was an error; and lastly (c) react only slowly in making sense of and reacting to the new circumstances.

Another historical footnote of strategic relevance: Hitler, showing surprising lack of nerve in view of the phenomenal success of the assault three days into the campaign, actually ordered General Guderian to halt his *Panzer* at the River Meuse to wait for the infantry to catch up. It would have been a major tactical mistake – one that quite possibly would have bogged down the German invasion in World War I-style trench warfare. Guderian knew that every day lost would give the Allies time to withdraw and regroup. He chose to defy Hitler's directives and acted in accordance with the nineteenth-century Prussian principle of *Auftragstaktik* (mission command) that confined headquarters to setting objectives while commanders in the field were given freedom to decide how best to achieve the objectives. Hitler subsequently awarded Guderian with a promotion to lieutenant-general for his boldness and initiative, despite his defiance of the *Führer*'s order. The question has been raised: would Guderian have gotten away with his defiance of an order in the British Army? Likely not. Roberts (2003)[5] has argued that this anecdote shows the persistent belief in Britain that German soldiers acted like automatons, blindly obeying orders, for the myth it is.

Returning to the *Nespresso* case, assumptions need to be carefully reviewed at the issues and sub-issues level. A simple example to illustrate the point: ecological sensitivities have changed over the past quarter century since *Nespresso* first launched its pod comprised of aluminum. While concerns over the recyclability of aluminum and energy consumption associated with its manufacturing have always existed, they were hardly mainstream in the early 1980s. That has changed. Assumptions regarding the acceptability of using aluminum containers to substantial segments of *Nespresso*'s markets need to be carefully reviewed. Competitors capable of providing alternative solutions (such as competitor Gaillard's bio-degradable version of the pod) have emerged and pose a potentially serious threat to *Nespresso*'s product offering.

Assumptions and the prevailing business logic must be continually challenged. Changing competitive environments invariably relegate assumptions that have been formed by past successes to obsolescence. Key success factors change as do conditions in the organization's markets. Whatever the source of the firm's strategic problems, organizations are well advised to examine these in light of their current business paradigm. Past successes are often the greatest hindrance to this exercise. Determinants of past success are all too often assumed to hold invariably for the future. Particularly in rapidly evolving competitive environments this is a perilous assumption. Even great industry players are prone to fail when led by obsolete industry logic.

Nowhere is this better illustrated than by the case of the American automobile industry. Take the case of General Motors (GM). Recently, Alex Taylor, an automotive journalist who has covered GM over that past thirty years, mused on its current woes.[6] Taylor suggests that CEO Rick Wagoner's most likely response to a question about why GM isn't more like Toyota would be: " . . . we are playing our own game – taking advantage of our own unique heritage and strengths". Given GM's current reality, however, it should have long since moved on and become more like Toyota. GM's rich heritage is of little use to it now. Its strengths – well, what are they? Toyota's market capitalization is $103.6 billion; GM's a rapidly diminishing $1.8 billion. In November and December 2008 alone GM required $4 billion to even stay afloat![7] GM provides a classic example of a misguided industry logic and obsolete intuition.

GM's situation hardly represents a precedent, however. It would appear that the automotive industry is particularly prone to misguided industry logic. Henry Ford's famous statement in 1922 that " . . . any customer can have a car painted any color that he wants as long as it is black" is testimony to the fact that even a pioneering visionary like Ford could end up missing obvious signs of changing consumer tastes. While his sturdy black Model T had made him rich, automobile buyers by 1920 were developing a taste for different cars and models. Ford's refusal to budge brought the Ford Motor Company to the brink of bankruptcy by the end of World War II. Toyota is a much more recent case in point. Its current difficulties in the face of its massive recalls have been attributed to its management's reluctance to believe the company could build faulty cars.[8]

STRATEGY IN PRACTICE: THE ROLE OF INTUITION IN FRAMING ISSUES

We will examine the role of intuition in strategy more thoroughly in the next chapter when we examine it in the context of sense making and the formation of insight. However, in the context of framing issues intuition also plays an important role. Intuition helps us frame views that in turn help us identify issues. Intuition also helps shape our assumptions. It draws on the subconscious and is linked to perception and insight, though it may be detached from any immediate conscious or rational deduction. Hence, it is so important that we take a few steps back every so often and challenge the views and perceptions that form the basis of our intuition.

Intuition expresses itself in a variety of ways. Whether we call it "gut feeling", *Fingerspitzengefühl*,[9] or a hunch, intuition is grounded in experience and derived from insights gained from reflection, learning and experiential knowledge, often gathered over a long period of time. Intuition can be very helpful in identifying and framing issues, particularly when these relate to complex contexts.

However, there is an important proviso to this: intuition is useful only if it is continually challenged and adapted to a continually changing reality. Intuition that fails to reflect current reality can be misleading at best. At worst, it can be fatal for the business when senior management fails to challenge its intuition and blindly adheres to obsolete industry logic.

Reality is highly complex. Numerous forces work inextricably alongside one another so that the effect and impact of any single factor remains inextricable. Synergetic effects between factors may trigger amplifications of outcomes in which the resulting impact is greater than the sum of its parts. Serendipity can also play a critical role, leading to probabilities of outcomes that simply cannot be computed. Problems arise when managers begin making seemingly convincing claims about the likelihood of the occurrence of these outcomes, when in reality it is impossible to establish any level of certainty concerning the likelihood of events.

Box 2.3 Black Swans and the Thanksgiving Turkey

In his recent bestseller, Nassim Nicholas Taleb[10] talks about "black swans", those highly improbable occurrences with potentially devastating impact. Examples of "black swans" include the September 11, 2001 terrorist attacks on the twin towers and the current global financial markets crisis. Taleb argues, for example, that contrary to conventional wisdom, almost none of the world's great discoveries were the result of design and planning. Rather, these were entirely serendipity-driven "black swans" and hence unpredictable.

Taleb elaborates on the dangers of making seemingly logical predictions about the future on the basis of assumptions that, in fact, bear no relevance to the ultimate occurrence. He illustrates this point by tracking the life of an American turkey up to the point of its fateful demise on the Wednesday before Thanksgiving. Nothing happening in the many days prior to the fateful day on which the turkey gets slaughtered could possibly prepare it for its ultimate surprise ending. The friendly daily feedings, if at all, reinforce the turkey's sense of well-being. In fact, one might imagine that the turkey's feeling of security is greatest when the risk has reached its pinnacle – on the day before the slaughter, the turkey's "black swan".

Taleb extends this illustration to general observations about the nature of empirical knowledge and our learning from past events – the notion that if something has worked in the past it may, in fact, turn out to be at best irrelevant, at worst fatally misleading in changing circumstances.

SUMMARIZING THE CHAPTER . . .

- Strategic questions represent the critical starting point of the strategic thinking process; they are triggered by trends, events or changes in the organization's competitive situation.
- They arise from the problems that these changing conditions trigger in the organization's ability to compete.
- Strategic questions that at any point in time have disproportionate business impact for the organization are relatively few in number; getting these few wrong, however, can have devastating implications for the organization's competitive position.
- Assumptions underpinning the prevailing business logic and paradigm must be challenged at this stage of the

strategic thinking process; this requires intellectual curiosity and willingness to abandon legacy recipes for success.
- Finally, articulating good strategic questions is only the starting point for the strategic thinking process.

Notes

1. Heisenberg, W. (1958) *Physics and Philosophy: The Revolution in Modern Science*, New York: Harper and Row.
2. The Pareto principle has been attributed to the Italian economist Vilfredo Federico Damaso Pareto (1848–1923) who observed that 80% of the income in Italy ended up with 20% of the population.
3. Schein, E.H. (1992) *Organizational Culture and Leadership*, 2nd ed., San Francisco: Jossey-Bass Publishers.
4. May, E.R. (2000) *Strange Victory: Hitler's Conquest of France*, New York: Hill and Wang; referenced in Light, P.C. (2005) *The Four Pillars of High Performance*, New York: McGraw-Hill.
5. Roberts, A. (2003) *Hitler and Churchill*, London: Phoenix, pp. 101–104.
6. Taylor, A. (2008) GM and Me, *Fortune*, 8 December, pp. 60–67.
7. Saporito, B. (2008) Is This Detroit's Last Winter? *Time*, 15 December, pp. 29–33.
8. References to Ford and Toyota were taken from Andrea Sachs' (2010) review of the newly released book in Richard S. Tedlow's book entitled Denial [London: Penguin] in *Time European Edition*, 175(12) (29 March 2010).
9. *Fingerspitzengefühl* translates literally from the German as "finger tip feeling" or the English expression "keeping a finger on the pulse"; it suggests an instinctive sixth sense; in a military context, this might be a field commander's instinctive grasp of an ever-changing operational and tactical situation on the battlefield.
10. Taleb, N.N. (2007) *The Black Swan*, London: Penguin; see also *The Independent on Sunday* (19 October 2008): The Visionaries: It's not Easy being Right, p. 10.

CHAPTER 3

Sense Making and Strategic Insight

Any fool can know. *The point is to* understand.

—Albert Einstein

IN THIS CHAPTER, WE:

- examine the role of sense making in the greater context of the strategic thinking process, explore some of the philosophical underpinnings of sense making and show how and why these matter;
- explore sense making from both the spatial and process perspectives:
  - in the spatial perspective we examine a framework for sense making that relates analysis, intuition and interpretation to the derivation of insight,
  - from a process perspective we examine how sense making occurs in complex organization contexts, and

> how it relates to learning, interpretation and the ascription of meaning in complex contexts;
> - close with a reflection on the formation of insight – the outcome of the sense making process.

Organizations and their competitive environments resemble a perplexing terrain. Our perceptions regarding that terrain are based on numerous inputs of information. Some of this information might be incomplete and unclear; some information might be outright misleading. That this is so has long been recognized in military contexts. The great Prussian military philosopher Carl von Clausewitz pointed out in his treatise *On War* that a "great part of the information obtained in war is contradictory, a greater part is false, and by far the greater part is of a doubtful character".[1] Some of the contradiction no doubt stems from the purely ambiguous circumstances encountered in war. Some, however, is deliberate. Deliberate distortion of information, or deception, has always played an important role in military strategy. In the military context, deception is about subtle manipulation and distortion of identity and purpose. This is used to influence the enemy's perception of reality and to instigate the enemy to act on their misperceptions. Green (2006) argues that in war, where the stakes are high, there is no moral stigma in using deception.[2]

The stakes in business environments, though of a different character, are no less high. As in war, we also encounter both deliberate and non-intentional ambiguity. Our perception of the ambiguity encountered may be subject to multiple and potentially conflicting interpretations, all of which may appear plausible from some point of argumentation. Kay (2010)[3] has argued that business organizations, being the complex political organizations that they are, tend to be influenced by individuals and groups with diverse and potentially conflicting agendas. Weighty and careful analysis of the rationale for decisions is most often possible only after these, in fact, have been taken into consideration.

Sense making is about creating coherence and order against this confusing backdrop of multiple possible "realities". The purpose of sense making is to introduce some degree of objectivity towards creating a better understanding of how events are linked; of the roles of actors and parties in complex competitive relationships.[4] It involves a deconstruction and reassembling of reality into bits of insight. Its purpose in strategy is to identify those insights that are most relevant to the problem or task at hand. In the strategic thinking context sense making is really an activity that takes place in the organization's realm of knowledge. It is part of the organization's higher-level knowledge and learning processes. While the underpinning theory falls broadly in the field of cognitive dynamics and is rich and deep in its own right, it is the purpose of this chapter to draw on only those elements that add insight to what the practitioner strategist needs to understand in the greater context of the strategic thinking process.

Much of what happens in organizations on an ongoing basis entails some element of sense making. Sense making takes on a particularly critical role in strategy. Sense making and formation of insight are fundamentally critical elements of the strategic thinking process. Schematically, sense making and the formation of insight are shown as a stage following the articulation of strategic questions and framing of relevant issues (Figure 3.1). Sense making is initiated in the stage in which issues are framed; issues, in turn, prompt insights to be generated through sense making.

Sense making involves a deconstruction of complexity through judicious combinations of analysis, intuition and interpretation. This process leads to the derivation of meaning in the specific context under examination. In a sense, it is a process that leads to the assembly of the relevant "bigger picture" or pattern. The

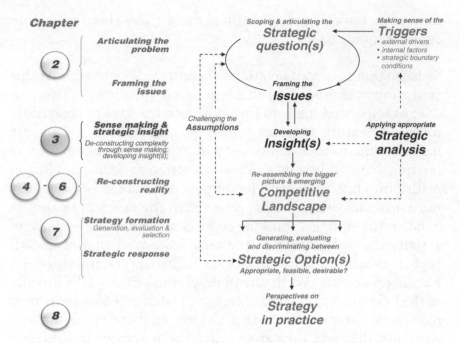

Figure 3.1 Sense making and formation of insight

objective of sense making is to establish a sufficient number of insights and to connect these in such a way that they create a coherent and connected, though inevitably incomplete, bigger picture. In the first section of this chapter we explore sense making; in the second part we examine the notion of insight.

Perspectives on Sense Making

Sense making has been dealt with from a variety of perspectives in the management literature. Philosophically, sense making is positioned between two contrasting views of how social science research should be approached. Two traditions, *positivism* and *social constructionism*, represent fundamentally different approaches to sense making. *Positivism* builds on the idea that reality exists in the external environment and is to be deduced through objective reasoning and measurement. In *social constructionism*, on the other hand, reality is derived through inferred interpretation of sensation, reflection and intuition. The tension arising between the two approaches in the context of sense making is explained by the respective differences in their *ontological* (relating to the philosophical assumptions about the nature of reality) and *epistemological* (relating to the general set of assumptions about the best ways of enquiring into the nature of reality) underpinnings.[5] Table 3.1 summarizes the fundamental differences. While the former leaves the analyst entirely out of the picture and aims to establish objective, causal explanations for circumstances and occurrences, the latter seeks to infer meaning and better understanding through reflection and interpretation of events and circumstances. Both approaches find application in sense making. Indeed, in sense making, we need contributions from both rational analyses as well as from intuition. This is why a

Table 3.1 Positivism and social constructionism: contrasting approaches to sense making and implications[6]

	Positivist approach	**Social constructionist approach**
Points of departure	Hypotheses	Meanings
Designs	Experimentation and deduction	Reflection and intuition
Techniques	Measurement	Discourse
Analysis	Verification of facts	Interpretation; derivation of meaning
Units of analysis	Reduction to simplest possible terms and elements	Seeks to capture complexity of the collective "whole"
Explanations	Must establish and demonstrate objective causality	Serve to increase overall general understanding of the situation
Outcomes	Causality	Understanding

pragmatic view that deliberately draws on both approaches for insight is the preferred mode in management practice.

Weick (1979;[7] 1995[8]) bases his perspective on sense making on a conceptualization of organizations as "loosely coupled" systems. Individuals play an important role in interpreting and assigning meaning to stimuli originating in the firm's external environment. Ultimately, though, the purpose of sense making is to reduce the equivocality of information in the organization's environment. Management thinkers Mintzberg *et al.* (1998)[9] and Choo (2002)[10] view sense making as contributing to the strategy process through its process of constructing meaning and the creation of knowledge. These subsequently lead to decision making that drives responsive action. This perspective is consistent with the *emergent* school of strategy thinking. Not entirely unrelated to this perspective, sense making has also been viewed as an organizational learning process by thinkers such as Nonaka and Takeuchi (1995),[11] Baumard (1999)[12] and others.

In this chapter we develop a dual perspective on sense making that draws mainly on the work of Weick, Mintzberg, and Nonaka and Takeuchi. We first explore sense making as occurring in an organizational *sense making space* as suggested in Figure 3.2. In the first section we briefly examine some of the elements contributing to the sense making process shown in Figure 3.2. This provides some insight on the individual parts, but not necessarily on how they collectively come together in the formation of insight. To build a better understanding of how these parts collectively contribute to sense making we then proceed in the subsequent section to explore the sense making from a *process* viewpoint as a second perspective. Sense making from this perspective is viewed essentially as an organizational learning process.

Though shown as a relatively systematic and orderly set of activities in Figure 3.2, the schematic at best reflects an approximation of what in reality consists of a highly complex and iterative process.

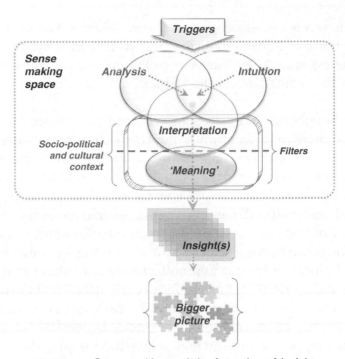

Figure 3.2 Sense making and the formation of insight

Sense Making: A Spatial Perspective

Organizations are often viewed as "black boxes". Constant and diverse inputs consisting of stimuli of all sorts are processed and transformed into action within the box. In the case of "black boxes" we see only inputs and outputs. A fundamental premise of this book is that organizations need not be viewed as "black boxes"; that managers in fact can and should play a central role in manipulating outcomes through informed action. In order to do so, however, they must be able to peer into and understand the inner workings of the organization. Sense making is a key element in that process.

To be clear, organizations are complex entities. We will never have complete understanding of their inner functioning, if only for the reason that organizations change continually and function at multiple levels not discernible to the visible eye. Hence, without any pretense of understanding of how it happens exactly, we can nonetheless surmise at least some elements of the sense making process that contribute to the formation of insight.

In very broad brush strokes, sense making is triggered by events, circumstances or other stimuli that threaten to change the status quo or perhaps offer new opportunities of some sort. Sense making then involves a combination of analysis, intuition and interpretation of the stimuli. These are shaped and filtered by the socio-political and cultural context within which the sense making occurs. Context determines our perception; the stimuli that triggered the sense making thereby attain meaning; meaning leads to bits and pieces of insight that collectively contribute to a bigger picture in the specific context of the events, circumstances or other stimuli that triggered the need for sense making in the first place. The outcome of the sense making exercise is insight leading to an image of a bigger picture. But how is insight formed – what actually happens in the "sense making" space that ultimately yields insight? We really don't know. We may assume that a significant part of sense making plays out at the subconscious levels of our thinking. At best we can observe the phenomenon.

STRATEGY IN PRACTICE: REFLECTIONS ON SENSE MAKING MECHANISMS

- Sense making, Clegg et al. (2008)[13] remind us, is what people in organizations do all the time, whether they are aware of it or not.
- Both individuals in organizations and organizations in the collective (for example, teams and groups) engage in this exercise through reflection and exchange of thinking and experiences.
- Organizations use a variety of mechanisms for sense making; analogies, mental models, metaphors, concepts and hypotheses can be very powerful mechanisms for capturing the spatial dimensions in organizational sense making.

- Nonaka and Takeuchi (1995)[14] discuss the critical role of such mechanisms in terms of quintessential knowledge creation processes that support organizational sense making; in this way, sense making is inextricably linked to the organization's learning processes (this is discussed in greater detail further on in this chapter).
- These mechanisms help to frame the numerous clues, cues and signals that are continually emerging in organizational contexts, some of which might be only short-lived; they enable us to "connect the dots", thereby helping us to frame our understanding within a greater rational context.

Insight has traditionally played a crucial role in the natural sciences throughout the ages. Insight in the form of "Eureka!" moments have brought forth important breakthroughs in scientific thinking, hence it is a logical field of endeavor to examine from a sense making perspective. Consider the following account of one such momentous event that resulted in Kekulé's discovery of the ring formula for the benzene molecule.

Box 3.1 Swirling Serpents and Molecules

The German chemist Friedrich August Kekulé von Stradonitz (1829–1896) had been puzzling over the structure of the six-carbon structure of benzene for some time. At the time it had been assumed that all organic compounds had an open chain of carbon atoms as backbone. Yet, a number of the properties exhibited by certain molecules such as benzene simply couldn't be accounted for by the prevailing assumption of a straight carbon chain structure. Kekulé's flash of insight occurred in a vision while he was dozing in front of the fire; this is his account of that momentous discovery:[15]

I was sitting writing on my textbook, but the work did not progress; my thoughts were elsewhere. I turned my chair to the fire and dozed. Again the atoms were gamboling before my eyes. This time the smaller groups kept modestly in the background. My mental eye, rendered more acute by the repeated visions of the kind, could now distinguish larger structures of manifold conformation; long rows sometimes more closely fitted together all twining and twisting in snake-like motion. But look! What was that? One of the snakes had seized hold of its own tail, and the form whirled mockingly before my eyes. As if by a flash of lightning I awoke; and this time also I spent the rest of the night in working out the consequences of the hypothesis.

What were the elements that ultimately contributed to Kekulé's flash of insight? We'll never know exactly, of course. Scientific research findings[16] recently published in the *Journal of Cognitive Neuroscience* suggest that although people may not be aware of it, their brains nonetheless have to be in a certain state of readiness in order for an insight to occur. The work reports, furthermore, that the state of the brain can be detected electrically several seconds in advance of the enlightening moment itself. Conscious thought, it appears, does not lead to insight; rather, unconscious processing happens in the background and only delivers the insight to the conscious once it has been arrived at.

In Kekulé's case we can safely assume that it was a combination of several factors – his factual expertise in chemistry, a lively imagination that played off his subconscious, and his ability to envisage three-dimensional shapes and forms in the abstract – which appears to have transpired in the subconscious at the critical moment. From a managerial perspective, we shouldn't overlook the importance of the setting: relaxed musing while snoozing in front of a fire. To think that napping on the job is still viewed as an infraction of the employment contract in most organizations!

Sense Making: A Process Perspective

How does sense making occur? In this section we begin by looking at how sense making is initiated. Several key elements of the sense making process are introduced. Next we look at the sense making process from several angles: we look at the role of interpretation and how this leads to the ascription of meaning; how it relates to learning. We then examine sense making in the context of complex organizational environments; in essence, we examine in the following sections those elements of sense making depicted in Figure 3.2.

Triggers

We've already looked at triggers in the previous chapter. We saw that, broadly speaking, these can be allocated to three areas: external drivers or stimuli, internal occurrences, or a combination of both. Sense making is triggered when there is a discrepancy between the assumed or expected, and what is actually encountered. Sense making is triggered by interruptions to ongoing routine activities. Weick[17] emphasizes the importance of novelty in triggering sense making: novelty might find its origins in dissonance, performance gaps, unanticipated disruptions, unexpected failure and uncertainty brought on by external events. These create the need for explanation. The purpose of sense making is to produce explanations for the novelty. In practice we talk about "reality checking". This proceeds through reciprocal interaction between information seeking and the attempt to ascribe meaning and causality.

Analysis

One of the formal sub-processes within the sense making space is pure rational analysis. It delivers a rational contribution to sense making. It can be assumed that this activity occurs largely in the conscious realm. It is predominantly a "left brain" activity that focuses on the objective analysis of facts, information and figures.

But this form of conscious sense making also includes the application of heuristics – simple rules of thumb or the deliberate application of lessons learned – which may have an element of experiential knowledge. Conscious, rational analysis deals mainly with codified, explicit stimuli. This may represent a limitation to sense making if only restricted to pure analysis since important intangible stimuli may be overlooked.

Intuition

Intuition is an ethereal sub-activity that occurs in the absence of any rational processes. Parikh *et al.* (1994)[18] suggest that intuition might be thought of as a process by which perception is formed on various levels of consciousness ranging from logical consciousness to the subconscious. Intuition is an internally experienced phenomenon that may also be influenced by external elements. Two components of intuition particularly relevant to sense making are the logical conscious and subconscious levels.

At the *conscious* level we find pattern recognition through rapid inference typified by "if . . . then" reasoning, the rapid retrieval of which occurs without the conscious application of logic or analysis. At the *subconscious* level the intuition process consists of tapping into the internal reservoir of cumulative experience and expertise developed over perhaps many years; distilling from this deeply embedded knowledge a response, insight or alternative without a conscious understanding of how we arrived at the particular insight. Sense making in practice draws on both the selective conscious mind and the more unorganized, holistic subconscious. Parikh *et al.* (1994) argue that sensitivity to resonances occurring from subconscious thought can be useful to our conscious thinking and can endow a subtle edge to our thinking. Subconscious thought draws on a vast amount of information that is largely disorganized and significantly more complex than that which we access in our conscious minds. We are consciously inhibited by what we perceive to be real whereas the subconscious encompasses the vast spectrum of the possible.

Intuition most effectively contributes to sense making when we are in a relaxed and reflective state of mind; when we relax, we momentarily suspend the deliberate organization of thought (such might also be the case when we engage in rhythmic physical activity such as jogging). This allows the subconscious to emerge in all its richness of experience and deeply embedded knowledge. New patterns and causal relationships between hitherto unconnected factors suddenly become apparent, much like Kekulé's flash of insight concerning the ring structure of the benzene molecule.

Interpretation and the Ascription of Meaning

Analysis, intuition and interpretation occur simultaneously in sense making space. Analysis and intuition provide data that subsequently needs to be interpreted for meaning. Weick (2001)[19] tells us that interpretation is that process by which inputs delivered to the organization (e.g. through analysis or intuition) are translated, developed into models for understanding and meaning, and put into context. Weick points out the role of the retrospective and "relating to" in sense making; that meaning is derived from experience and association with the known often only after the fact. As a social activity, sense making is a process in which people co-create, or enact their environment through discourse, conversation and the narrative. In engaging in these activities, people notice, extract, and embellish cues; these are the familiar structures from which a larger sense of what is occurring is then derived. Finally, not surprisingly, Weick describes sense making as a process that involves emotion and that might provoke confusion.

The meaning derived through interpretation may be strongly influenced by the sociopolitical or cultural context within which the interpretation occurs. We differentiate between *high* and *low* context settings. *High context* settings are characterized by internalized, "closed-society" and implicit understanding of values, norms and communication. Knowledge is relevant largely "here and now"; it is situational and relational. *Low context* is universal, rule-oriented and based on codified knowledge that is transferable and widely applicable. Sequencing of time, space, activities and relationships is separated in low context settings.

Context shapes sense making; contexts impose filters on interpretation that reflect the sociopolitical and cultural attributes of the environment. A specific context may even result in a gross "distortion" of sense making in certain settings and circumstances as the example in Box 3.2 illustrates.

BOX 3.2 TRIAL BY RED-HOT IRON[20]

Picture the scene: Röthenbach in the Black Forest in the year 1485. An assembly of clergy at the signorial court of the Count of Fürstenberg. A woman accused of witchcraft has been arraigned before the signorial court. The Count has decided to place the matter of justice in the hands of God. The suspected witch is to be subjected to the "trial by red-hot iron" ordeal. The accused, by this procedure, is required to take a red-hot iron from a furnace and carry it for three paces. The suspect's hand would then be bound for three days upon which the wound would be inspected. A cleanly healed wound would lead to a declaration of innocence; a weeping or discolored wound would be grounds for condemnation. The woman accused of witchcraft submits to the trial with confidence (not that she is given much choice in the matter). According to one account, she carries the glowing iron not only for the stipulated three paces; she carries it for six. She is eventually acquitted and freed. In a strange twist of justice, the case is brought to the attention of the two Dominican friars Heinrich Krämer and Jakob Sprenger, who condemn the verdict in their influential treatise on witchcraft entitled

Malleus Maleficarium (1486) on the grounds that the procedure is potentially open to demonic manipulation – conceivable on the grounds that the devil, a master of natural science, may have protected the woman's hand by invisibly placing something between her hand and the hot iron. Judges are warned to avoid using the ordeal in future trials.

Making sense of this case in a modern societal and judicial context leaves us shaking our heads. The woman is first accused of a crime now regarded as impossible (was it possibly her red hair that had triggered the persecution in the first place?) and then set free by a process that appears entirely arbitrary and random. Were her judges irrational, their attitudes and behavior derived from stupidity or hysteria, or possibly a combination of both? Evidence gathered by scholars of medieval and Renaissance history suggests otherwise. Writings from this period indicate an extensive and high level of learning. Even the allegations against witches – suggesting they congregated at night to kill infants and worship the devil – are found in the writings of scholars who rooted their works in the Bible and the philosophy of the Church fathers. The practice of the ordeal, until its decline in the thirteenth century, was endorsed by some of the most thoughtful and scholarly Christians in Western Europe.

Sense making is shaped by sociopolitical and cultural context. Have we made significant and substantial progress in our sociopolitical and culture thinking and practices since the middle ages? In many ways we have, indeed; nonetheless we needn't look far in some organizations today to find examples of outcomes of "sense making" that, while not carried to the extreme described in this case, leave us shaking our heads no less.

Sense making as described in the illustration (Box 3.2) often goes hand in hand with what Baumard (1999)[21] describes as a *territorialization* of knowledge and cognition in organizations (or even societies) driven in part by the bounded rationality of key actors, but also in an effort to protect their knowledge which they associate with their power and authority.

Sense Making and Learning

Sense making serves to help identify bits and pieces of strategically relevant information related to a particular strategic problem; to sort and filter these and reassemble them into bundles of insight that might be relevant to that particular problem. In so doing, it is an activity that involves both conscious analysis and intuition in creating order, sorting out paradox, and making retrospective sense of situations in which the organization finds itself.[22] Ideally, sense making is a collective activity, involving interaction and discourse amongst individuals in the organization.

STRATEGY IN PRACTICE: SENSE MAKING AND SOME BASIC UNDERLYING ASSUMPTIONS

We draw on Weick (2001)[23] for a summary of some of the basic assumptions underpinning the notion of sense making:

- Sense making is about interpreting reality which is ongoing even as we try to make sense of it; sense making is about capturing flows, a continually changing environment, variations in choice and irrevocability in an organizational context that is evolving even as it makes sense of itself and its environment.[24]
- Sense making is a retrospective process; reminiscing a primary source of derived meaning.
- Symbols and symbolic processes are central features of the sense making exercise; they help associate conscious

and subconscious ideas, thereby endowing meaning and significance to complex phenomena.

- Sense making draws on images and maps to help rationalize complex relationships; these in turn help establish plausible patterns that support the interpretation of complex reality.
- Ultimately, sense making is a mechanism for reducing equivocality (multiple meanings) of an ambiguous context into a more manageable and relevant set of meanings (Daft and Weick, 1984[25]).
- Sense making can be viewed as a learning process in the complex environment of an organization.

Sense Making in Complex Environments

The greater the complexity of an organizational context, the greater we expect the demands on sense making to be. But what do we mean by *complexity*? What is *complexity* in a business context? Though we intuitively understand what the term implies, complexity is actually difficult to define. The original Latin word *complexus* infers things that are entwined or twisted together. This suggests that complexity involves numerous elements linked in some intricate arrangement. The component elements may be events as such or parties external to the organization. In an organizational context complexity relates to the importance which tacit structures and processes play in the functioning of the particular organization in question. That is to say, complex organizations depend heavily on interactions and transactions within the organization that are not readily obvious to the casual observer.

It has been suggested that organizations can be viewed as intricate interpretation and sense making systems,[26] whereby interpretation and sense making occur in three stages (Baumard, 1999):[27]

1. *Scrutiny* against a complex combination of signals, stimuli and impulses;
2. *Conferral* of meaning to the information thus gathered; and
3. *Translation* of this information to actionable knowledge by way of organizational learning.

A number of organizational learning theories have been proposed for explaining how these stages actually happen in organizations. Generally these theories draw on sociocultural psychological perspectives of the organization in which learning involves socially mediated cognitive processes of interpretation and sense making. These theories seek to explain the roles of the individual as well as that of the collective in this process. One of these is the *SECI* (*Socialization, Externalization, Combination and Internalization*) model proposed by Nonaka and Takeuchi (1995). Their model emphasizes the social nature of organizational learning; it explains how knowledge is transformed between the tacit and explicit knowledge modes.

Nonaka and Takeuchi's framework reflects a Japanese perspective that views the organization as a living entity that encompasses a collective sense of identity and purpose – as opposed to a typically Western view of the organization as a machine. Perhaps what lends it particular credence for sense making is that it accounts for intangible as well as the more readily visible tangible elements. Sense making can be viewed as one of the multiple knowledge processes explained by the *SECI* model. This framework furthermore identifies appropriate enabling conditions that support organizational sense making:[28]

1. *Intention* ensures the strategic underpinning of the sense making process, linking the purpose of the activity to value creation.
2. *Autonomy* ensures the appropriate flexibility in acquiring, interpreting and relating information through a system of

"minimum critical specification", thereby setting parameters for internal sense making.

3. *Fluctuation/creative chaos* ensures appropriate stimulation of the interaction between the organization and its external environment, thereby setting parameters for making sense of external factors.

4. *Redundancy* supports internal organizational knowledge processes by provision of information that might go beyond the immediate requirements of the organization, but which may be relevant in the future.

5. *Requisite variety* ensures sufficient variety of information to match the organization's internal diversity and the complexity of its external environment; seeks also to reduce any information differentials across the organization.

Although Nonaka and Takeuchi's knowledge creation process begins with the individual, learning is viewed as occurring largely in teams – in an organizational collective sense. Personal knowledge becomes available to the organization through appropriate transformation mechanisms.

Tovstiga *et al.* (2005)[29] have proposed a framework for sense making that draws on Baumard's model of knowledge transitions, the Nonaka and Takeuchi *SECI* model and the *Intuiting-Interpreting-Integrating-Institutionalization* (*4I*) framework of organizational learning of Crossan *et al.* (2003)[30] to suggest how sense making occurs in an organizational context (Figure 3.3) through interaction between the organization's individuals and the collective, and the organization's tacit and explicit processes.

Intuiting is associated with the highly tacit process of pattern recognition on the basis of individual's deep expertise in a field. This is the capability, for example, of an expert to recognize a pattern in a problem that a novice may not. Often this reflects deep expertise acquired over many years of practice. At the root of intuiting is the process of transferring explicit knowledge into

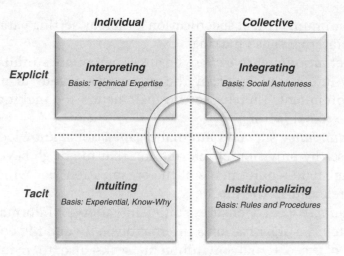

Figure 3.3 Sense making in an organizational context

tacit knowledge. Experiential knowledge is internalized by the individual in the form of shared mental models and know-why.

Positioned in the upper left quadrant, *interpreting* is the process by which individuals share and explain insights on the basis of their own knowledge and expertise. They do so through words and actions; these may be in the form of metaphors, analogies, concepts, hypotheses or models. Differences in perceived reality and experiential context within an organization, however, may lead to potentially conflicting situations. This is sometimes observed in post-merger integration phases when the merging organizational cultures clash. Interpreting is a quintessential knowledge-creation step, occurring largely through externalization.

Integrating, positioned in the upper right quadrant, is associated primarily with developing shared understanding and taking coordinated action through mutual adjustment. Knowledge sharing occurs through social interaction; group dialogue and storytelling. New tacit knowledge such as shared mental models may emerge from this learning interaction. This mode of knowledge creation is most often associated with the theories of group processes and sociocultural interaction. It is also associated with the evolution of social astuteness.

Finally, *institutionalizing* ensures that accepted knowledge and insights are embedded in the organization. Institutionalizing involves combining different bodies of explicit knowledge. This process may support the operationalization of a visionary strategy, product concepts and organizational routines and procedures. The process may involve explicating written instructions or embedding unwritten rules. Institutionalizing contributes significantly to the formalization of an organization's identity.

Mintzberg *et al.* (1998)[31] lend support to this view; they suggest (with reference to Figure 3.3) that *intuiting* is a subconscious (*tacit*) process occurring at the level of the individual and that this represents the start of the learning process. *Interpreting* then follows on the conscious (*explicit*) elements of the individual learning and from the individual to the collective while transitioning through a group level positioned between the individual and the organizational collective (featured in the Crossan *et al.* model), where *integrating* of the explicated insights changes the collective understanding. Finally, *institutionalizing* embeds that learning in the firm's collective memory, an expression of which might be found in the organization's corporate culture.

STRATEGY IN PRACTICE: SENSE MAKING IN THE ORGANIZATIONAL CONTEXT

Organizational contexts represent complex settings for sense making. Various factors contributing to the complexity of this task have been discussed in the preceding section. Sense making, however, is a critical organizational mechanism for generating strategic insight. Weick (2001)[32] proposes the following seven practical questions for fathoming the organization's wherewithal for sense making:

- *Social context:* Does the organizational context encourage conversation?

- *Identity:* Does the organizational context provide its people with a definitive sense of who they are and what they represent?
- *Retrospect:* Is there sufficient data to reconstruct past events; how quickly does the organization "forget" past relevant events?
- *Salient clues, cues and evidence:* Does the organizational context enhance the visibility of important inputs to its sense making process?
- *Ongoing projects:* Does the organizational context encourage overall continuity even in the event of interruption?
- *Plausibility:* Does the organizational context encourage coherent and credible reflection and exchange relating to events?
- *Enactment:* Does the organizational context encourage action or hesitation?

Box 3.3 Cultural "Branding" at Bayer AG

[**cultural:** *with reference to the complex of typical behavior or standardized social characteristics peculiar to a specific group, occupation, profession . . . ;* **branding:** *to mark with a brand; a mark of a simple easily recognized pattern made by burning with a hot iron . . . "; based on* Webster's Third New International Dictionary]

Organizations deal with their cultures in different ways. Legacy-rich companies tend to nurture strong corporate cultures. I am reminded of my early days in the venerable *Zentrale Forschung* (central research laboratory) of Bayer AG in Leverkusen, Germany. A freshly minted chemical engineering PhD, I was joining what was at the time one of the largest industrial research laboratories in Europe. The year was 1986 and Bayer was still an archetypal German industrial behemoth deeply entrenched in the "Rhineland Model" mindset.

One of my more poignant impressions from those early days was being informed by one of the mentors charged with my cultural induction that considerable effort would be invested by the company over the next five years on my assimilation into the "Bayer family"; an experience, he added – and this only half in jest – that would essentially amount to being "branded" with the iconic "Bayer cross" (Germans tend to have a way with vivid imagery). What was being implied? Several things. I was being groomed for a life-long career with the company. People joined Bayer anticipating employment for life. It was to be a comfortable life. Bayer was intent on fulfilling its commitments to its employee stakeholders; excellent pay, benefits that included world class health care and on-site clinics, and perks such as low interest-rate mortgages for home owners, a strong commitment to work–life balance and a strong corporate identity to cement company loyalty on the part of the employees. *Bayer '04*, its sponsored premier league football team, was only one of Bayer's many indulgences.

The model had worked well over the years. Loyalty to "the Bayer" was often expressed in terms of years and generations a family had worked for Bayer. Job mobility in the prevailing German context meant rotation within the Bayer Group. Part of the grooming involved an organizational cultural indoctrination; part was an ongoing management development training since German companies at the time developed their own management resources (MBAs were then largely unknown in German industry). The company was prepared to invest five years of what was expected to be a 30 or more year career with the company. Bayer's "cultural branding" was not left to chance; it involved a rich blend of mandatory events including corporate initiation rituals and off-site cultural induction seminars. But it also included rigorous in-house managerial training in subject areas such as financial management carried out in week-long seminars at *Kaderschmieden* such as the *Universitätsseminar der Wirtschaft* at *Schloss Gracht*, a management training academy funded and shared by a consortium of German industry conglomerates housed in a medieval castle not far from Cologne.

Cultural integration, alignment of mindset, and the embedding of Bayer's legacy values and norms were at stake. Bayer's rich legacy: its stories – for example, Bayer chemist Felix Hoffmann's discovery of Aspirin in 1897; its not entirely uncontested role in the Second World War IG Farben industrial complex; its post-war re-emergence as Bayer AG and its phenomenal growth and success – all these were part of the rich corporate tapestry that formed the backdrop of the company's identity and culture. In short, in true loyalty to its stakeholders, Bayer provided all that was required for a fulfilling life-long career. In return, the company expected reciprocal loyalty from its employees.

Little wonder then that my decision to leave the company after five years triggered mostly puzzlement among colleagues; expressed in thinly veiled whispers: " . . . how can you possibly leave 'the Bayer family' after only five years?" From a very few, however, I also heard: " . . . good thing you're leaving now, leave while you still can; . . . wish I'd have left 10 years earlier; I could no longer now!"

Insight Formation

Sense making leads to the formation of insight. Competitive differentiation gained by an organization begins with unique insight. Pietersen (2002)[33] argues that the battle for superior insight is really the starting point of competitiveness. Insight has been defined as the clear or deep perception of a situation; the often sudden understanding of a complex situation, or grasping the inner nature of things intuitively.[34] Insight is the outcome of the sense making process, which in turn is closely related to the organizational learning process. Prahalad and Bettis (1986)[35] suggest that organizational sense making leading to insight occurs via a process that draws on pre-existing knowledge systems and mental models – or schemas. The authors suggest that schemas are made up not only of legacy-related beliefs, theories and values, but that they are also influenced by the organization's objectives since these in turn influence the sort of information the organization accumulates.

Mintzberg *et al.* (1998) suggest that while the source of insight may remain mysterious, its presence is not. It is an ability to grasp the deeper meaning of an issue and how this issue fits into the bigger picture alongside other fragments of insight. Insight draws on skills other than pure analytical reasoning. In fact, much of what leads to insight cannot be verbalized and lends itself more to images and spatial abstraction, as we are reminded by Kekulé's experience (Box 3.1). Insight thereby is arguably much more an outcome of right hemisphere activity than a left brain exercise. Mintzberg (1994)[36] suggests as much in his reflection on what he refers to as the "soft underbelly of hard data" and the limited use of hard data for forming insight:

- Hard data is limited in scope and simply does not encompass the richness of non-quantifiable economic factors.
- Often hard information loses much of its strategic relevance through aggregation and simplification.
- Much hard information lacks immediacy; it is simply not available when needed most since it takes time to become available.
- A lot of *hard* information is surprisingly unreliable; it is subject to biases and distortion through processing.

STRATEGY IN PRACTICE: SENSE MAKING AND ITS LIMITATIONS IN ORGANIZATIONS

Clegg *et al.* (2008)[37] argue that many strategic errors originate with managers' false perceptions of the limitations of their sphere of influence in managing outcomes; they are indicative of deficiencies in understanding and utilizing the outcomes of sense making in the organization:

- Many managers still approach strategic decision making by relying on tools and planning procedures that assume the world represented by these is as controllable and as rational as these might suggest.
- Outcomes are much more determined by the success of sense making in the organization – and the degree to which sense making contributes to a shared and common understanding against a backdrop of diverse factors.
- Sense making seeks to bring into juxtaposition different interests, disciplines, knowledge backgrounds and power relations – and ideally contributes to reconciliation of these within organizations.
- When strategies fail, it is often through the failure of managers to recognize the organizational context for what it really is: a highly politicized and contested setting prone to irrational behavior on the part of its members.

SUMMARIZING THE CHAPTER . . .

- Sense making seeks to create meaning and insight from both explicit and tacit knowledge and information.
- It draws as much on analytical reasoning as it does on intuition, hunches and other "soft" inputs that constitute integral elements of tacit knowledge.
- Often, the latter embody the more critical and relevant inputs to the sense making process.

- The collective set of inputs largely defies traditional mechanistic approaches to their analysis because of the intangible nature of important inputs.
- Therein resides the managerial challenge of sense making: how does one create and nurture the right organizational context and culture for sense making to occur most effectively – an environment conducive to deep reflection, trust, collective sharing of insights, experiences and knowledge, and learning?

Notes

1. von Clausewitz, C. and Green, J.I. (2003) *The Essential Clausewitz: Selections from "On War,"* Mineola, NY: Dover Publications.
2. Greene, R. (2006) *The 33 Strategies of War*, London: Profile Books, p. 305.
3. Kay, J. (2010) Inquiry – You're Getting Warmer . . . , *Financial Times* (FT.COM Magazine), 352 (20/21 March).
4. Weick, K.E. (2001) *Making Sense of the Organization*, Oxford: Blackwell Publishing.
5. Easterby-Smith, M., Thorpe, R. and Jackson, P.R. (2008) *Management Research*, 3rd ed., London: Sage.
6. Ibid.
7. Weick, K.E. (1979) *The Social Psychology of Organizations*, 2nd ed., New York: Random House.
8. Weick, K.E. (1995) *Sensemaking in Organizations*, Thousand Oaks, CA: Sage.
9. Mintzberg, H., Ahlstrand, B. and Lampel, J. (1998) *Strategy Safari*, New York: The Free Press.
10. Choo, C.W. (2002) Sensemaking, Knowledge Creation, and Decision Making, in Choo, C.W. and Bontis, N. (eds) *The Strategic Management of Intellectual Capital and Organizational Knowledge*, Oxford: Oxford University Press.
11. Nonaka, I. and Takeuchi, H. (1995) *The Knowledge-Creating Company*, Oxford: Oxford University Press.
12. Baumard, P. (1999) *Tacit Knowledge in Organizations*, London: Sage Publications.

13. Clegg, S., Kornberger, M. and Pitsis, T. (2008) *Managing &* *Organizations*, London: Sage.
14. Nonaka, I. and Takeuchi, H. (1995) (note 11 above).
15. Horvitz, L.A. (2002) *Eureka!: Scientific Breakthroughs that Changed the World*, Chichester: John Wiley & Sons Ltd.
16. *The Economist* (2009) Incognito (16 April – from the print edition).
17. Weick, K.E. (2001) (note 4 above).
18. Parikh, J., Neubauer, F. and Lank, A. (1994) *Intuition*, Oxford: Blackwell Business.
19. Weick, K.E. (2001) (note 4 above).
20. Taken from: Oldridge, D. (2007) *Strange Histories*, London: Routledge.
21. Baumard, P. (1999) (note 12 above).
22. Weick, K.E. (2001) (note 4 above).
23. Ibid.
24. DeFillippi, R. and Ornstein, S. (2003) Psychological Perspectives Underlying Theories of Organizational Learning, in Easterby-Smith, M. and Lyles, M.A. (eds) *Handbook of Organizational Learning and Knowledge Management*, Oxford: Blackwell Publishing.
25. Daft, R. and Weick, K.E. (1984) Toward a Model of Organizations as Interpretive Systems, *Academy of Management Review*, 9 (2), p. 284.
26. Ibid.
27. Baumard, P. (1999) (note 12 above).
28. Nonaka, I. and Takeuchi, H. (note 11 above).
29. Tovstiga, G., Odenthal, S. and Goerner, S. (2005) Sense Making and Learning in Complex Organisations: The String Quartet Revisited, *International Journal of Management Concepts and Philosophy*, 1 (3), pp. 215–231.
30. Crossan, M.M. and Berdrow, I. (2003) Organizational Learning and Strategic Renewal, *Strategic Management Journal*, 24, pp. 1087–1105.
31. Mintzberg, H., Ahlstrand, B. and Lampel, J. (1998) (note 9 above).
32. Weick, K.E. (2001) (note 4 above); (in this reference, the author makes further reference to Weick, K.E. (1995) (note 8 above) for more details on the seven properties of sense making).
33. Pietersen, W. (2002) *Reinventing Strategy*, New York: John Wiley & Sons, Inc.
34. Webster's Online Dictionary [www.websters-online-dictionary. org/].

35. Prahalad, C.K. and Bettis, R.A. (1986) The Dominant Logic: A New Linkage between Diversity and Performance, *Strategic Management Journal*, 7, pp. 485–501.
36. Mintzberg, H. (1994) *The Rise and Fall of Strategic Planning*, New York: The Free Press.
37. Clegg, S., Kornberger, M. and Pitsis, T. (2008) (note 13 above).

CHAPTER 4

Insight-Driven Strategic Analysis

*All models and frameworks of analysis are inherently flawed;
some are nonetheless useful.*
—Overheard in the Silicon Valley

IN THIS CHAPTER, WE:

- critically reflect on the process underlying strategic analysis; its purpose and role in sense making and the generation of insight;
- introduce a typology consisting of a hierarchy of frameworks of strategic analysis based on high-level and supporting-level frameworks of analysis;
- describe the roles of high-level and supporting-level frameworks of analysis;

- propose a simple step-by-step approach to conducting an insight-driven strategic analysis;
- review and discuss the limitations of strategic analysis.

Strategic analysis is about sense making. It is about making sense of those elements in the firm's environment that are relevant to its current and future competitive position. These elements might be external to the firm, such as the emergence of new opportunities or possibly threats. They might also relate to factors internal to the firm, such as its ability to meet those new opportunities or threats. Most often it is a combination of external and internal factors that trigger the need to sense making. To that end, strategic analysis is central to the strategic thinking process a firm needs to engage in on a continual basis in monitoring and nurturing its competitive position.

Clearly, however, in order for strategic analysis to be competitively relevant it needs to be purposeful; the purpose of sense making is to generate insights derived from external and internal factors that when suitably aggregated are relevant to the ability of the firm to compete successfully. Hence, the outcome of strategic analysis should enable the firm to make better decisions in response to the salient competitive questions: *where* to compete, *how* to compete, and *when* to do *what* in pursuing new opportunities or fending off threats from competitors. The question of *why* we want to compete at all in any given context is another important consideration. In essence, the strategic analysis through sense making should provide appropriate responses to the questions posited by the five building blocks of strategy discussed earlier in Chapters 1 and 2.

Strategic analysis as shown in Figure 4.1 serves at least three purposes in the strategic thinking process. First, it serves to make sense of the triggers that prompted the need to revisit the firm's strategy in the first place. It does so by guiding the framing of the

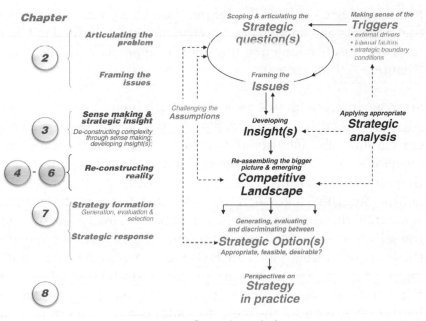

Figure 4.1 Strategic analysis

relevant strategic issues and the formulation of suitable strategic questions from these. Second, strategic analysis provides guidance to the generation of the insights elicited by the strategic questions framed in the preceding stage. Astute questions prompt insights that are strategically relevant. Invariably, not all strategically important questions posed can be answered at any one point in time; this has to do with the complexity and ambiguity of real business environments. However, as argued in the previous chapter, rigorous sense making will nonetheless enable the firm to identify those insights that are critical and relevant to the situation at hand. Third, strategic analysis provides guidance in piecing together the individual bits and pieces of insight into an aggregated "bigger picture" on the basis of which strategy formation can proceed. In this way, strategic analysis involves sense making (deconstructing of complex, real contexts), the generation of insight, and the reconstruction of the reality relevant to the firm's strategic context. Therefore, with reference to Figure 4.1, the concepts and approaches to sense making described in Chapter 3 are closely coupled to the analysis approaches dealt with in Chapters 4 through 6.

Strategic analysis draws on a multidisciplinary combination of rigorous scientific and informal processes that are used to derive correlations, and identify and evaluate trends, patterns and performance gaps. It is used to identify and evaluate opportunities as they emerge in an organization's competitive environment. It guides our thinking when we assemble the various insights generated through analysis and intuition. Finally, it supports the selection and evaluation of appropriate strategies for pursuing those opportunities. Good analysis requires reliable data – and a lot of practice. The more one practices strategic analysis, the more proficient one becomes. Strategic analysis, properly done, is hard work. It is one of the more difficult tasks a strategist is called upon to do.

Strategic analysis has fallen under considerable criticism in management circles in recent years. The management consulting industry is at least partially at fault for this. Strategy consultants have been particularly proficient at releasing a deluge of tools, methodologies, frameworks and techniques of analysis onto the market. There are literally hundreds of tools and techniques of analysis available today. However, the maxim "rubbish in, rubbish out" holds here as much as it does elsewhere.

In view of the competitive reality facing almost all organizations today – that of unprecedented and irreversible change in competitive environments resulting in ever decreasing time horizons – most approaches relying solely on rational strategic analysis are no longer adequate. All frameworks of strategic analysis simplify reality to some degree through the introduction of assumptions. For example, many of the frameworks of strategic analysis currently in use are limited by their implicit or explicit assumption that industry boundaries are constant and well defined; moreover, they presume that organizations know exactly who their competitors, suppliers and customers are. In the past these assumption may have been valid to some extent in some industry sectors. Today, however, these assumptions are obsolete in virtually all industry sectors. The smartphone sector provides an apt illustration: the smartphone industry emerged from a convergence of three formerly distinct sectors – telephones, media and computing. Its trajectory had its origins in the conventional mobile telephone industry (where *Nokia* had established a strong foothold), but it rapidly encompassed media platforms driven by new entrants (such as *Apple* and its *iTunes* platform), and has now moved on beyond the actual gadget to where the competition is on operating systems, driven by another new entrant (*Google* and its *Android* operating system).

Even in cases in which frameworks demonstrate validity over a limited range of parameters, poor data – whether obsolete, incomplete or simply irrelevant – may render these useless. Data may also be deliberately misused. The practice of managing on the basis of performance ratios is a case in point. Take the ratio *"return on equity"* or *ROE*. Many companies desire a better return on their equity. So, what could be wrong with that? Managing for *ROE* was standard practice at Lehman Brothers. Ultimately it turned out to be the firm's undoing. Lehman Brothers is no more because managing for *ROE* encouraged its management to over-borrow, even when the first indicators of an economic recession appeared on the horizon. Debt in bad times does not earn returns as it does in good times. It isn't equity. Lehman ignored this fact. It practiced extreme leverage by shrinking the ratio's *E* in the denominator recklessly low. In doing so, Lehman tweaked its numbers and paid its executives according to that measure. Managing for the wrong ratio caught up with the company in a fatal way. Many other ratios such as gross margin and earnings per share are equally prone to misuse. It is relatively easy to make them look good while damaging the business's true business bottom line.

Box 4.1 Of Models and Men

The recent financial crisis that began in 2007 has dealt a devastating blow to the credibility of analytical models and theories used in the prediction of financial market performance. One in particular, the *"efficient-markets hypothesis"* or *EMH*, has come under sharp criticism. Its essence – the price of a financial asset – reflects all available information that is relevant to its value. Wall Street came to draw powerful conclusions from this relatively straightforward assumption. What it implies is that if the *EMH* holds, then markets will price financial assets correctly, and deviations from equilibrium will not last long. Ideas such as the *EMH* coupled with the complex mathematics that describes them have given rise to the Wall Street profession of "financial engineering". A number of financial products emerged over the years from the ensuing effort: derivatives and securitizations, ever more intricate credit-fault swaps and collateralized debt obligations. It was thought at the time of their appearance that these inventions were making the financial markets safer and the economy healthier. Only gradually did skeptics begin questioning the validity of the models. Fact of the matter is that the vast majority of derivative contracts and securitizations have performed precisely as their models predicted they would. It has been argued that exceptions triggered the financial catastrophe.

So what went wrong? Myron Scholes, who won the 1997 Nobel Prize for his contributions to the Black-Scholes formula for pricing options (one of the most widely used models in the finance industry), has argued in defense of the *EMH* by pointing out that *"there are models, and there are those that use the models"*. The problem in Scholes' view is not with the validity of the models, rather the way in which they were used by Wall Street and the City (London's financial community). Financial analysts fed the models with data that incorrectly suggested conditions that were much more benign than they were in reality. The models moreover inherently assume that markets behave rationally.

Behavioral economists, who apply the insights of psychology to finance, have been particularly skeptical of the markets' inherent rationality. Not only do humans behave irrationally, particularly in the face of losses, they have argued, people tend to be overly confident of their own abilities and tend to extrapolate recent trends into the future – thereby extending the applicability of the models used far beyond their intended range of validity.

The debate is far from over, though. To date, no new model has emerged to replace the *efficient market hypothesis* paradigm. And behavioral economics has yet to provide evidence for how it affects prices. What we do see once again is that it is not the models, but the human factor that introduces the risk through irrational behavior and faulty judgment.

Perhaps new approaches that integrate analysts' research findings into the forecasting algorithms of the computer-driven stock-trading models, but are void of the biases and emotions that can influence trading decisions, will address the current deficit. Whether or not these and other new advances that succeed in balancing rational and behavioural inputs to analysis and decision making will prove to provide a better paradigm remains to be seen. Hopefully, we will not need another financial meltdown to answer that question.

Sources: 1. *The Economist* (2009) Financial Economics: Efficiency and Beyond (18 July 2009); 2. *The Wall Street Journal* (2012) A Twist on "Quant" Trading: Weave in Analysts' Research (contributed by Jenny Strasburg, 23 May 2012).

Arguably, though, much of the criticism against strategic analysis has been misplaced. The fault really doesn't lie with analysis, but rather with its misguided application and the blind faith that many managers attach to it. Managers find comfort in numbers – anything "hard" to justify an important decision, even if the numbers are largely irrelevant. We need to remember that all frameworks are inherently flawed by virtue of their oversimplification of reality which is ambiguous and complex. This does not render them useless, but it does hold implications for how we use them. Moreover, not all frameworks are equally useful. A number of frameworks still in circulation are on the verge of obsolescence. New ones are continually emerging.

We argued earlier in this section that strategic analysis needs to be purposeful; by extension, the choice and application of frameworks of analysis need to serve the purpose of the analysis. Suitably selected and applied, frameworks of strategic analysis can shed light on a small part of the complex reality of the situation in question. When these perspectives are collectively integrated and appropriately aggregated we begin to see a pattern emerging. This pattern, though incomplete, provides an approximation of the bigger picture. However, when combined with informed intuition and skilled interpretation, even an approximation derived on this basis may be adequate for strategic decision making. The real skill in strategic analysis thus lies in (1) beginning with the "right" strategic questions, (2) in the choice and application of appropriate frameworks of analysis for sense making, and ultimately, (3) in the integration and aggregation of the insights thereby generated towards reconstructing the firm's competitive reality in terms of a useful strategic landscape. The firm's competitors face the same challenge, of course. Hence the real challenge in strategic analysis lies in the combined skill and speed with which the firm succeeds in "cutting to the chase" with regard to making sense of its competitive environment in a way that enables it to respond more quickly to change than its competitors.

Thus, frameworks of strategic analysis can help guide and support our thinking, but they will never replace it. Despite the abundance of frameworks in the management literature, relatively few suitably selected and properly applied can yield a lot of insight. This is not suggesting that we ignore the complexity of a business context. It is suggesting, however, that it is how we make use the frameworks that matters. Most often, the limitations are not even related to the frameworks per se, rather to the validity and reliability of the data on which assumptions made for the analysis are based.

Box 4.2 Beyond the "Dimon Principle"

Not having access to validated and proven hard evidence is a reality often encountered in business. Insight-driven strategic analysis is challenging under these circumstances. Strategic decisions demand to be made nonetheless. Different industry sectors deal with this dilemma in different ways. Financial services appear to have been particularly prone to engaging in high risk ventures with a predilection that has been both naïve and surprisingly brash.

J.P. Morgan Chase, currently the US's largest bank by assets, emerged from the recent economic meltdown relatively unscathed. But it is now facing its own version of a corporate meltdown; it provides a prime example of the gullibility large established institutions can fall prey to. Initially waved off as a "tempest in a teapot" by its chief executive, James Dimon, its fiasco ended up as a $2 billion trading loss. In disclosing the news of the loss at a hastily organized news conference on 10 May 2012, Dimon furtively suggested that the trading that led to the fiasco had "violated the Dimon principle". He did not elaborate on the meaning of the "Dimon principle". Perhaps, just as well. If J.P. Morgan's dealings in the past are any indication, at stake may be its tendency to letting complex risk run unfettered, and not countering prevailing sector logic with arguments that might have challenged and disproved J.P. Morgan's own beliefs.

Richard Feynman, the Nobel Prize-winning physicist, formulated a simple alternative principle that Dimon would have been wise to heed: "*You must not fool yourself – and you are the easiest person to fool.*" Closely associated with unchallenged assumptions is wishful thinking. In a commencement address delivered to a Caltech audience in 1974, Feynman made reference to the "cargo cult" of Pacific islanders, who believed that they could make airplanes bearing food and clothing land simply by lining up alongside makeshift airstrips as they had during the Second World War.

J.P. Morgan Chase and similar institutions deploying techniques such as the "value at risk", or VAR technique that is used to estimate the potential vulnerabilities of their investment decision making are well advised to remember that "the riskiest moment is when you are right", in the words of economist Peter Bernstein. British philosopher and social critic Bertrand Russell pointed out that " . . . *the less evidence someone has that his ideas are right, the more vehemently he asserts that there is no doubt whatsoever that he is exactly right*". Fact of the matter is that we often do not have the evidence we require, but this demands that we proceed all the more cautiously in circumstances lacking hard data; possibly by applying a "*pre-mortem*" – a technique proposed by psychologist Gary Klein: (1) soliciting advice from people whose views you respect; (2) asking them to reflect critically by imagining looking back a year from now, on a disastrous investment you have made; (3) asking them to list all the possible causes leading to the failure. And finally, not forgetting " . . . that the smarter you are, the more easily you can fool yourself".

Source: The Wall Street Journal (2012) Forget the Dimon Principle and Try the Feynman Rule (contributed by: Jason Zweig, 14 May 2012).

The greatest benefit derived from using frameworks of analysis relates to the clarity they can contribute to the thinking process. Often it's not about the actual output of the analysis, but rather the focus and structure the frameworks can bring to the debate on the topic at hand around the boardroom table. Senior managers more often than not lack good listening skills; they are prone to take out of a discussion only what they want to hear. In such situations, even the simple act of bringing something to paper or the white board in a structured way can help immensely in channeling meaningful debate and moving the collective thinking forward in the right direction.

Getting Started: High-level and Supporting-level Frameworks of Strategic Analysis

How does one most effectively approach setting up a strategic analysis? Where does one begin? How does one avoid "losing sight of the wood for the trees"? In this section we examine a typology for frameworks of strategic analysis that addresses these questions (Figure 4.2). The typology structures frameworks into two levels of analysis. The first, a *high-level* analysis, provides a view of the "bigger picture" that integrates both external and internal factors; importantly, it does so in the context of the specific value offering that is at the core of the strategic challenge that prompted the analysis at the outset. In doing so, the high-level perspective focuses the strategic analysis on the core strategic consideration at stake – that of creating and delivering a unique and superior value offering to its relevant stakeholders. Moreover, this level of analysis probes the strategic boundaries of the opportunity space representing the firm's competitive position and thereby offers a powerful means of structuring the thinking of the analysis around the core of the strategic challenge in question. We will be examining two high-level frameworks of analysis – the *value proposition* and the *unique competing space* frameworks – in Chapter 5.

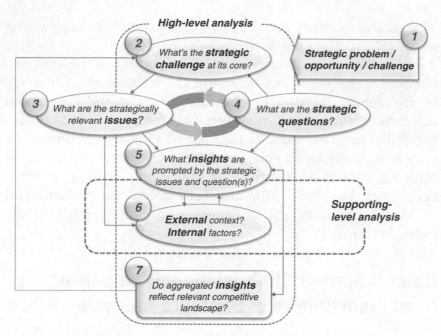

Figure 4.2   Insight-driven strategic analysis: high- and supporting-level analyses

The supporting level of analysis draws on frameworks of analysis that selectively provide depth of analysis on either external or internal factors. Supporting-level frameworks of analysis can provide useful *contextual* insight – insight on either external competitive contexts or internal firm contexts that reflect the organization's basis of competitiveness. Examples include the *key success factor analysis*, *industry maturity analysis*, or a *strategic resources audit and analysis*.

The two levels of strategic analysis are not interchangeable. Both serve a specific purpose. Most often, it makes sense to begin a strategic analysis with a scoping of the strategic challenge on the basis of a high-level analysis. Students and managers most often encounter difficulties when they attempt to go straight into a supporting-level analysis rather than first scoping the greater strategic context with the help of a high-level analysis.

Setting Up and Conducting a Strategic Analysis

Reputedly, many roads lead to Rome. Nonetheless, not all are recommendable; some roads may, indeed, turn out to be dead ends. Similarly, there are numerous conceivable approaches to strategic analysis. Not all, however, lead to useful insight. There are those that easily lead astray, and there are those that "cut to the chase" and thereby leave less room for straying from the task at hand. The general approach described in the following is based on the schematic shown in Figure 4.2; it identifies key steps and the questions that need to be addressed at the various stages of the analysis. Subsequent Chapters 5 and 6 then focus the high-level and supporting-level frameworks of analysis, respectively.

The first step (see numbering of steps indicated in Figure 4.2) in conducting a strategic analysis consists of identifying and scrutinizing the problem (which might be an opportunity or challenge) for scope and relevance. It is important at this point to ensure that the problem (or challenge) is indeed strategically relevant and that its resolution is worth pursuing; that it, indeed, justifies the effort that is to be spent on it.

The second step is an extension of the first step. Its purpose is to probe the strategic relevance of the challenge to be analyzed and to establish its link to the firm's competitive position; its relevance to the value offering at stake. The third and fourth steps are iterative; their purpose is to frame the issues and, ultimately, the strategic question (or questions) that are to be explored in the analysis. Both the articulation of strategic questions and the framing of issues analysis have been dealt with in Chapter 2. For the purpose of strategic analysis a broad clustering of issues, for example, in matters relating to the external competitive context and those relating to the firm's internal basis of competitiveness, can be helpful in achieving some degree of structure at this stage of the analysis. Generally, strategic questions emerge from a convergence of associated issues. Step 5 builds on the outcomes of the issues framing and articulation of the strategic questions. Issues and questions prompt insights. Insight, we argued in Chapter 3, is a key input into sense making. The foregoing issues analysis throws open questions that prompt insight. Not all questions can be answered for various possible reasons. Competitive environments, we have argued in earlier chapters, are ambiguous and complex; potentially critical insights are often not available or accessible. Hence, an important part of this step is to determine which insights are required, which are available and possible implications for the strategic analysis arising from those insights not available. Insights are generated through application of appropriate supporting-level frameworks of strategic analysis that focus on either the external or internal contexts (step 6). The nature of the insights required determines which frameworks are selected and where the emphasis of the analysis is to be – whether on external or internal factors. At an advanced level of analysis the objective is to achieve a high level of integration between the various frameworks used in the analysis. We will examine how this is done in Chapter 6. Finally, in the seventh and last step of the analysis process, insights are aggregated and integrated in a way that enables the reconstruction of the bigger picture relevant to the strategic challenge at hand. As we have argued in earlier chapters, real competitive contexts are ambiguous, fluid and continually changing. Hence, we will never get the "complete" picture; however, if astutely conducted the strategic analysis can provide us with a sufficiently "realistic" assessment of the strategic context relevant to the challenge at stake to enable appropriate decision making.

STRATEGY IN PRACTICE: SIMPLE STEPS IN SETTING UP AN INSIGHT-DRIVEN STRATEGIC ANALYSIS

1. Starting with a relevant challenge . . .
   - What is the challenge – is it a problem to be resolved, an opportunity to be captured, a threat to be countered?
   - Why is it a problem – and for whom?

- How does it manifest itself?
- Who are the stakeholders who stand to gain (or lose) by its resolution (or failure to achieve resolution)?
- How will its resolution make any difference to the competitive position of the firm; what is the expected impact?
- What would be the potential cost of simply ignoring it?

2. Scoping the strategic dimension of the challenge . . .
   - What is the strategic element at the core of the challenge?
   - How does it relate to the firm's competitive position; its ability to defend or create a uniquely superior value offering?
   - What is its potential strategic impact (temporal, spatial, etc.)?

3. Framing the strategic issues . . .
   - What are the strategic issues associated with the strategic challenge?
   - What makes them "strategic"; how do they relate to the strategic challenge at stake?
   - How might these be linked, and how might issues be clustered in a meaningful way (e.g. those related to the external; those related to internal factors)?

4. Articulating the strategic questions . . .
   - What are the (relatively few) questions that cut to the core of the strategic challenge at stake?
   - How (and why) will resolution of these make any difference to the challenge at hand?

5. Identifying the insights prompted by the strategic questions . . .
   - What insights are prompted by the strategic questions?
   - Does the issues analysis enable a broad clustering of insights – and how might this structuring of insights contribute to a better understanding of the issues related to the challenge at stake?

- Which insights are potentially important but cannot be accessed or generated?

6. Extricating the insights: external and internal contexts . . .
   - What are the external and internal factors relevant to the strategic challenge – which insights can be extricated from these factors?
   - Which are the appropriate frameworks of analysis and what insights do these contribute to the analysis?
   - Which factors are linked; how might an integration of insights derived from appropriate frameworks of analysis contribute to a better understanding of the strategic challenge?

7. Consolidating and aggregating the insights . . .
   - How valid and reliable is the competitive landscape that emerges from the analysis?
   - Is it relevant to the strategic challenge that prompted the analysis in the first place?
   - What parts are missing; how critical are the missing pieces?
   - What potentially important insights are missing or simply not accessible?
   - What are the implications and the potential impact of the missing insight(s) for strategic decision making?
   - Do the aggregated insights reflect the competitive landscape of the relevant strategic challenge?

SUMMARIZING THE CHAPTER . . .

- Strategic analysis, purposefully structured and executed, can contribute powerful inputs to the strategic thinking process and the creation of insight.
- Frameworks of strategic analysis can be useful in creating insight if appropriately selected and applied; some are

more useful than others; some still in circulation are essentially obsolete.

- There are no limitations to the sophistication of frameworks and models of strategic analysis in circulation today; however, ultimately all are limited by the validity and reliability of the data used in the analysis.
- A few, relatively simple frameworks appropriately applied and integrated can generate powerful insight.
- Often the greatest value generated by the application of frameworks of strategic analysis lies not so much in their specific outputs, but rather in the focus and structure they can contribute to the debate and dialogue around the boardroom table.

CHAPTER 5

Strategic Analysis II: High-Level Sense Making

If you can't explain it simply, you don't understand it well enough.

—Albert Einstein

IN THIS CHAPTER, WE:

- examine the purpose and role of high-level strategic analysis in strategic sense making;
- introduce two high-level frameworks of strategic analysis – the *value proposition* and *unique competing space* frameworks – and discuss their application toward generating strategically relevant insight;
- examine how these high-level frameworks can guide the overall strategic process through aggregation and integration of a number of individual approaches, models and frameworks;

- close with a final analysis framework, the *opportunity-response* framework, which addresses the "when?" question related to strategic scheduling.

The purpose of high-level strategic analyses is to probe and map the firm's strategic position in its greater competitive context. Central to the firm's strategic position is its ability and disposition to create and deliver a uniquely superior *value offering* to its relevant stakeholders. Hence we begin this chapter with a short reflection on the strategic value imperative. We then examine two high-level frameworks of strategic analysis – the *value proposition* framework and the *unique competing space* framework. These frameworks represent structured, high-level approaches to strategic analysis. The two frameworks are complementary, and importantly, both converge on an expression of the value offering that is at the core of any strategic analysis. Moreover, as high-level analyses, the *value proposition* and *unique competing space* approaches are comprehensive; they collate and integrate a number of supporting frameworks of strategic analysis – and, importantly, they bring these into the context of the core strategic consideration at stake: the firm's relative competitive position.

The power of the high-level analyses derives from the structured guidance they contribute to the strategic thinking process. Appropriately applied they help guide the sense making process from its inception (i.e. asking the right strategic questions) through to the piecing together of a reconstructed "big picture" view of the company's competitive landscape. Ultimately, this level of analysis focuses attention on the essence of an organization's competitiveness. This might be its relative position to where opportunities for value creation and delivery exist, its current competitive position in delivering that value, or an indication of the strategic direction required to achieve that objective.

Toward that end, the high-level strategic analysis comprehensively addresses the firm's salient strategic questions – the *"where"* do we want to compete; the *"how"* do we want to compete; the *"what"* in terms of value offering at the core of the strategic differentiation; and the *"why"* do we want to compete at all?

We close the chapter with an examination of a third framework, the opportunity-response framework, which while not explicitly focusing on the *"what"* does address the time dimension, that is, the *"when"* question.

The Strategic Value Imperative

Strategy, we have argued earlier, is about *winning*. Firms compete by differentiating themselves from their competitors in the way in which they create, bundle and deliver value offering. The recipients of this value offering are the firm's stakeholders. Firms "win" by creating and delivering a uniquely superior *value* offering to their stakeholders. This is the firm's strategic value imperative. As we might imagine, the firm's stakeholders may represent a diverse group of people and constituents; their expectations of the value to be delivered may be equally diverse; these may range from highly tangible returns (such as a dividend on stock held by a shareholder) to highly intangible expectations (such as customer experience in a services transaction). The latter form, though difficult to quantify, is no less important than the former measurable form of value. In fact, we are seeing an increase in emphasis on intangible forms of value. It is the creation and delivery of a superior value offering, regardless of its form, to its stakeholders that comprises the core purpose of the firm. The notion of "value" thereby takes on a key role in strategy. The two high-level frameworks of strategic analysis represent structured approaches to coming to terms with this key strategic objective.

Value Proposition (VP) Concept, Framework and Analysis

The notion of the *value proposition* as a formal concept is a relatively recent development in the field of strategic management. This is not to suggest, however, that successful firms have not understood and put to practice its basic tenets in the past. Strategy thinkers such as Peter F. Drucker,[1] Gary Hamel and C.K. Prahalad[2] laid the groundwork for the formalized concept of the value proposition in the early 1990s. Drucker's classic *Harvard Business Review* paper "The Theory of Business" is especially insightful. It derives the firm's theory of business in terms of three input elements; in Drucker's terminology these take the form of basic *assumptions* regarding the firm's (1) *external competitive environment*, (2) *internal basis of competitiveness*, and (3) *core purpose* and *aspirations*. The role of managers is to continually challenge the firm's assumptions in these three areas. He argues further that together these assumptions form the basis of the firm's *strategic intent*. Drucker's *theory of business* correlates closely with what we now refer to as the *value proposition*. The value proposition finds its articulation in the strategic intent – which in its simplest form is an expression of the firm's unique and superior value offering.

The value proposition is insightful not only as a strategy concept. It also provides the basis for a powerful high-level framework of strategic analysis. The elements of the value proposition framework derived from the concept are presented schematically in Figure 5.1, which indicates the three basic input elements in Drucker's *theory of business*; these are overlaid with the questions *"where?"*, *"how?"* and *"why?"* in respect of a firm's engaging in business. These culminate in the *"what?"*, which as an expression of the value proposition is essentially an articulation of the firm's *strategic intent*.

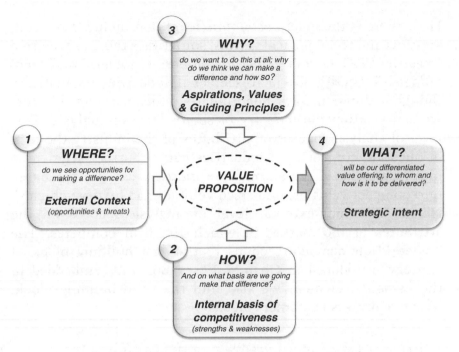

Figure 5.1 Value proposition concept and framework

WHERE (are the opportunities for value creation and possible threats to our ability to do so)?

The first of the inputs (labeled "1" in Figure 5.1) to the value proposition focuses on assumptions regarding the "where?" question. These probe the *external competitive environment* of the firm. The "where?" element challenges the firm's assumptions regarding where it sees opportunities for creating and delivering a unique and differentiated value offering – and how these opportunities might be changing. External competitive environments represent not only opportunities, they can also harbor threats to the firm's competitive position; hence this element also probes where and wherein these might lie, and possible implications for the firm. The external competitive environment of the firm can be structured in several levels.

First, there is the *macro-economic* level that includes societal, political and technological factors; sometimes these are referred to as the PEST factors (*political, economic, societal and technological*). These global factors affect all industries and markets, though in different ways. Subordinate to the macro-level factors we can position the *industry* or *sector* level of analysis. This level of analysis focuses on attributes of the industry the firm in question competes in. Industries can be further segmented into *markets* (e.g. the automotive *industry* can be segmented into compact vehicles, mid-sized vehicles and luxury vehicles). Hence, the final external level of analysis focuses on the attributes of the market in which the firm competes. The *"where?"* element corresponds to the first building block of strategy introduced in Chapter 1 (see Box 1.2). Embedded in the *"where?"* element we also find the third building block, which addresses customers' needs.

HOW (are we going to create and deliver the value offering)?

The second input component (*"2"* in Figure 5.1) of the value proposition, the *"how?"* question, focuses on the *internal basis of competitiveness*; it challenges the firm's assumptions regarding what it needs to excel at in order to create and deliver a uniquely superior value offering. Hence it probes the firm's ability to create and deliver a superior value offering to its stakeholders. These assumptions address primarily the firm's resources and capabilities and the firm's *uniqueness* and *superiority* in the way it combines, reconfigures and exploits these towards creating a uniquely differentiated value offering. By extension, the *"how?"* question also addresses the firm's organizational context; its structure, processes, practices and ability to align these effectively. In the broadest sense, the *"how?"* question probes the firm's strengths and weaknesses; how these might be changing, and possible competitive implications for the firm. This element of the value proposition corresponds to the second building block of strategy (Box 1.2).

WHY (are we in this business at all)?

The third and final input element ("3" in Figure 5.1) to the value proposition, the "*why?*" question, probes assumptions regarding the firm's *aspirations*, its *guiding principles* and *values*. It challenges the firm's assumption on what the firm considers meaningful results, how it envisions making a difference through its value offering, and its motivations for doing so.

The "*why?*" element provides the rationale that underpins the firm's "*how?*". It probes the organization's intrinsic disposition towards creating value. It captures the firm's passion, aspirations and the higher purpose of its (ideally) unique calling to the task at hand. This element of the firm's value proposition is the most subtle one and, arguably, also the most sustaining one. External contexts addressed by the "*where?*" question can change very rapidly; internal contexts captured by the "*how?*" also change, though generally less rapidly due to organizational inertia. However, the "*why?*" is least prone to change. It can, however, change over the years. Firms such as Intel (from memory chips to microprocessors), IBM (from mainframe computers to personal computers to services) and Nokia (from forest products to telecommunications) are examples of firms that have experienced fundamental transitions in their conception of why they are in business.

Together, the three inputs converge to define the fourth element in the value proposition framework (element "*4*" in Figure 5.1) as an output; the firm's *strategic intent*.

WHAT (is our differentiated and uniquely superior value offering)?

The value proposition is a powerful means of harnessing the firm's strategic aspirations – its *strategic intent*. This finds expression in the "*what?*" question – which elucidates the uniquely superior value at the root of the firm's differentiated offering. It clearly stakes out the benefit of that value offering for the various stakeholders, whether these are customers, employees, shareholders, or indeed, society at large. It says as much about where the firm will focus its efforts as it does about where it will *not* focus effort.[2] The firm's articulation of its value proposition finds expression in its *strategic intent.* The strategic intent captures the essence of a firm's strategic aspirations by collating the firm's assumptions regarding the *where*, *how* and *why* relevant to the firm's differentiated value offering. Moreover, the strategic intent introduces an element of *stretch* to the firm's value proposition by recognizing that there may be a gap between the firm's current reality (its current ability to fulfill its value proposition) and what it aspires to be. In doing so, the strategic intent continually challenges the organization by creating a pretext for the competitive position it aspires to achieve.

The strategic intent also addresses the mode and format in which the differentiated value the firm creates is delivered. The mode in which a firm creates its value offering and the format in which the firm delivers it relates to its *value disciplines.* As proposed by Treacy and Wiersema (1995),[3] *value disciplines* can take on one of three possible dimensions – *operational excellence, product leadership,* and *customer intimacy.* Which value discipline a firm focuses on depends largely on its industry and the nature of competition in that industry. *Operational excellence* is typically associated with mature or commodities-based industries, in which cost pressure demands focus on reduction of operating cost. *Product leadership* pertains mainly to industries focusing on high value-added markets such as luxury goods and bespoke product/service offerings, in which innovation, brand and value attributes other than price provide potential for sizable margins. *Customer intimacy* is characteristically the focus of the value discipline in the service industries. In these, the value exchange takes place in a transaction involving a strong relational component. Management thinking on the notion of value disciplines has evolved since its introduction. Most managers today recognize that a value offering does not necessarily fall neatly into any single value discipline. A firm's value imperative often demands delivery of a value offering in a way that suitably fulfills unique combinations of value disciplines.

Unique Competing Space (UCS) Framework and Analysis

One thing that sets industry leaders apart from less successful competitors is their strategy. They do not leave it to chance. Competitive advantage, when achieved, is invariably an outcome of deliberate effort. Firms that succeed in gaining competitive advantage continually strive to achieve clarity with regard to their competitive position, difficult as this might be in real business contexts. They seek to understand the determinants of their unique window of opportunity for creating value – their *unique competing space,* and they continually monitor the *boundaries* of their unique competing space as their competitive context evolves. This enables them to preemptively take appropriate strategic action when this is called for.

How might we better understand the firm's unique window of opportunity on creating and delivering value? What is the firm's *unique competing space* and what are its *strategic boundaries?* Why are they so critical? How can a better understanding of these help in identifying ways of achieving competitive advantage? These are the questions we address in this section.

The Firm's "Unique Competing Space"

A firm's competitive position can be viewed in various ways. It can be a competitive stance; for example, the firm's position in relation to its competitors. Alternatively, it can be the firm's domain within which it is advantageously positioned to create and deliver a uniquely superior and thereby differentiated value offering. Recent management thinking is focusing on this latter perspective. Collis and Rukstad[4] refer to the firm's opportunity space for creating a uniquely differentiated value offering as a *"strategic sweet spot"*. This is the competitive domain in which the company succeeds in meeting customer needs in a way that its rivals cannot. This space, once established for the firm, is competitively interesting for a number of reasons. First, it sets the firm clearly apart from its competitors. This has important implications for the firm's reputation; this, in turn, has consequences, for example, for the firm's ability to build its brand, attract talent, credit, and thereby gain access to new markets. Second, a *unique competing space*, once established, has important economic pricing implications. It sets the firm apart from its competition in respect of its ability to price its value offering at a premium by virtue of the uniqueness and superiority of that value offering.

Geometrically, this is shown in the schematic in Figure 5.2 as the triangular space straddling the spheres labeled *"3"* and *"4"*. Clearly, this is a spatial domain rather than a one-dimensional point as might be suggested by Collis and Rukstad's reference to a

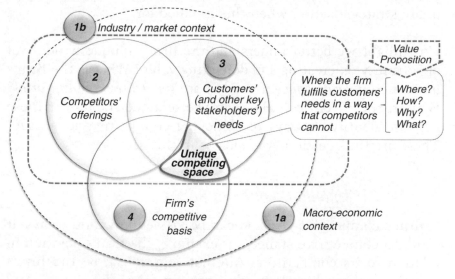

Figure 5.2 The firm's unique competing space

"sweet spot". We therefore refer to this domain as the firm's *unique competing space* in this book. The spatial character of the domain in question, we will see, has very important strategic implications; as a spatial domain, the firm's *unique competing space* is bounded by three interfaces representing the competitive (or *strategic*) boundaries of the firm, each of which carries critical implications for the firm's competitive position.

Nomenclature aside, the notion of the domain is powerful. The firm's *unique competing space* is the domain in which the firm creates and delivers a value offering in response to customers' needs in a way that competitors cannot. The *unique competing space* portrays this domain schematically; the *value proposition* substantiates the essence of the unique and superior value offering suggested by the domain. The conceptual rationale underpinning the firm's *unique competing space* rests on multiple clusters. Three of the clusters (*customers' needs, competitors' offerings,* and *firm's competitive basis*) are interlocked in a relationship depicted by a Venn diagram. These three clusters are enclosed by perimeters representing the firm's macro-economic and industry/market environments (Figure 5.2).

Box 5.1 Novo Nordisk's Unique Competing Space

Novo Nordisk is unique among pharmaceutical manufacturers today. Its bigger rivals have sought to restructure through mergers and acquisitions, or to diversify into vaccines and animal health in view of expiring patents. Novo Nordisk has stayed its course – and has seen its sales grow at double-digit rates and healthy operating margins of about 30%. Novo Nordisk is in the business of producing drugs that treat diabetes; it is already the world's biggest maker of insulin.

The potential competing space is lucrative. Few diseases hold greater promise for commercial returns in the coming years.

Diabetes, a chronic condition requiring lifetime treatment, currently afflicts some 180 million people worldwide. The World Health Organization estimates that number to double by the year 2030. A number of factors are contributing to that: an ageing population and a rising incidence of obesity in the rich top the list. Novo Nordisk has been investing effort in finding new treatments for type 2 diabetes; a condition that develops in adulthood when overweight people become desensitized to the insulin the body produces naturally. This is also the most prevalent form of the disease. Insulin, being a natural product, is not patented. However, drugs that stimulate its natural production in the body can be patented. This, and in the area of more effective insulin formulations, is where Novo Nordisk sees its unique competing space. Its *Victoza* type 2 drug, which is currently under review for approval in the USA, will face competition from other drug manufacturers' products also in last-stage trial. However, most type 2 patients eventually end up having to take insulin – and Novo Nordisk remains the world's leading producer of insulin. This positions Novo Nordisk uniquely: it can fulfill the needs of a growing population of diabetes patients in a way in which its competitors cannot.

Source: Financial Times, The Lex Column (Friday, 30 October 2009).

The Firm's Macro-Economic and Industry/ Market Environment

The *macro-economic environment* (labeled "*1a*" in Figure 5.2) represents all those factors in the firm's macro-environment that are of relevance to its competitive position – with the exclusion of those factors represented by two specific elements (*customers' needs* and *competitors' offerings*, both of which, strictly speaking, are also external factors from the firm's perspective). The macro-economic factors represented by the outer circle correlate with those macro-level factors discussed in the context of the value proposition in the previous section. A secondary external environment represented by the rectangular boxed region (labeled "*1b*" in Figure 5.2) narrows the focus of the analysis to the firm's *industry and market level*. It is important to remember that factors representing the firm's external competitive context, on whatever level, cannot be influenced by any individual firm; firms must, nonetheless, continually monitor and assess the strategic implications of changes in their external environment.

Competitors and Their Offering

The cluster in Figure 5.2 (labeled "2") representing the *competitors' offerings* narrows the focus of the analysis on the firm's competitors. In this cluster we find all those industry and market players who, alongside the firm, are vying to fulfill the value needs of customers in the relevant market. The constitution of the group representing the firm's competitors may be diverse; we may find established players as well as new entrants and emerging competitors. In the central domain formed by the overlapping of all three circles we find all competitors who find themselves in a position to fulfill customers' current needs to some degree. Needless to point out, this is a hotly contested space. Analyses that provide insight into competitors' abilities and activities, and the nature of the competition, are of relevance in this space. As in the case of the macro-economic analysis, snapshot analyses are useful; trend analyses that track changes over time provide potentially much more powerful insights.

Customers and Their Needs

Customers' needs are represented by a further circle in Figure 5.2 (labeled "3"). Strictly speaking, this circle represents the greater community of stakeholders, which, for example, in a public sector context might include beneficiaries and constituents. Customers represent one particular stakeholder group. Generally, whether customers or stakeholders at large, this group represents the recipients and consumers of the value created and delivered by the firm and/or its competitors, in return for which they generate economic returns. Critical insights for the firm include: Who are my customers? What are their needs? How are these changing? The point is, the identity of customers is not always clear; their needs even less so. Customers at times don't really understand their own needs and how these are changing. Hence, it is important for the firm to be close to its customers, to anticipate customers' needs when these emerge and to be agile in delivering on these.

The Firm and its Basis of Competitiveness

The lower circle in the Venn diagram shown in Figure 5.2 (labeled "4") representing the firm's competitive basis encompasses not only its resources (physical and financial) and capabilities (representing its intellectual capital), but also the greater organizational context embodying the firm's structure, processes, practices, culture and leadership. Therefore, this circle represents the basis on which the firm competes, its *competitive wherewithal*. The perspective prompted by this representation of the firm's competitive position prompts a critical premise: the fact that the firm possesses resources and capabilities does not necessarily mean that it is successful in exploiting these in a way that makes them relevant to its unique competing space, that is, in a way that enables the firm to derive competitive advantage from them. In order for this to be the case the firm must ensure that it succeeds in transferring its resources, capabilities and practices across the interface and into the domain representing the *unique competing space*. We will explore this very important implication in greater detail further on in this chapter.

Box 5.2 SIMPLICITY AND THE BEAST

Management scholars have long pondered over the trade-off between simplification of complex contexts and the consequences associated with the potential loss of contextual specificity. Complexity in business environments from a firm's perspective can be viewed as a result of interaction between the various elements that comprise the *unique competing space*, and more particularly, define its boundaries. The recent economic crisis has only added urgency to the question. Typically, businesses deal with complex competitive contexts by introducing ever more complexity to their own internal business routines under the assumption that this is an appropriate countermeasure. Organizations have a natural tendency to become more complex, not less. In practice, this introduces ever more inertia to the organization's ability to react swiftly to external change. The business rationale behind simplifying internal complexity, therefore, is compelling. "Simplifying and replicating" is a basic tenet promulgated by management thinkers Zook and Allen in their recent book *Repeatability*. Complexity, they argue, is the silent killer of modern business. Successful companies, the authors argue, share the following three virtues: (1) they focus on a highly distinctive core business; (2) they keep their business model as simple as possible; and finally (3) they relentlessly pursue new opportunities to replicate this model.

Companies cited by the authors adhering to these virtues include *IKEA*, *McDonald's*, *Lego* and *Apple*. One might argue that the virtues proposed by Zook and Allen, indeed, encompass key factors for enhancing the *unique competing spaces* these companies have succeeded in securing for themselves. According to the authors, these companies have made a cult of simplicity and replication. Apple CEO Tim Cook, for example, has been quoted to say:

"We believe in the simple, not the complex; we believe in saying no to thousands of projects so that we can really focus on the few." So, it would appear that the success of these companies corroborates their obsession with simplicity and their ability to replicate.

However, if the foregoing appears to be just a little too formulaic, it might well be that it is just that. *The Economist*'s "Schumpeter" throws a countering thought into the ring: just how do simplicity and repeatability help deal with disruptive innovation? The counterargument continues by pointing out that many once successful companies like *Kodak*, *Nokia* and *Blockbuster* did not succumb to complexity or an inability to "repeat". *Nokia*, indeed, *championed* repeatability with clear business models, a distinctive business model and a commitment to global rollout of its products. Nonetheless, in June 2012 this company had its credit rating downgraded by Moody's to "junk bond" status amid further announcements of headcount reduction bringing total jobs cut to 10,000 worldwide.

So, what is the lesson to be learned?

Formulaic approaches are to be enjoyed with caution. They often isolate individual elements that don't capture the entire story. *Nokia*'s failure to anticipate the market impact of a new entrant (*Apple* and its *iPhone*) had arguably little to do with a lack of ability to simplify and repeat. *Nokia*'s dilemma, illustrated with the help of a *unique competing space* perspective, points to difficulties stemming from an inability to counter multiple change on all three of its strategic boundaries; changes in the *competitors' offerings*, changes in the *customers' needs* and, not least, inability to counter these effectively on the basis of its *competitive wherewithal*. Most companies can normally handle serious issues arising at any single strategic boundary without too much difficulty; issues arising simultaneously at two boundaries are a significantly greater challenge for firms. *Nokia*'s current problems arise from significant simultaneous change at all three strategic boundaries. No amount of simplification and replication stand to placate this beast.

Sources: 1. Zook, C. and Allen, J. (2012) *Repeatability: Build Enduring Businesses for a World of Constant Change*, Boston: Harvard Business School Press; 2. Simplify and Repeat, Schumpeter, *The Economist* (28 April 2012); 3. *BBC Business News* (2012) Moody's Agency Downgrades Nokia Bonds to "Junk" Status (http://www.bbc.co.uk/news/business-18460636; accessed 5 August 2012).

The Unique Competing Space; the Value Proposition and Strategic Growth

Not surprisingly, the notion of the firm's *unique competing space* is intrinsically linked to the notion of its *value proposition*. The value proposition articulates the strategic rationale that substantiates the firm's *unique competing space*. Schematically, the *unique competing space* represents a geometric mapping of the firm's competitive position; conceptually, it represents the opportunity space underpinning its competitive position. Both notions, the *unique competing space* and the *value proposition*, are intrinsically linked to strategic growth. There are several good reasons for this: the existence of a *unique competing space* substantiated by a uniquely superior *value proposition* signifies that a firm has the potential for growth. So-called "growth companies", firms perceived to have growth potential, are viewed and valued favorably by key stakeholders, whether Wall Street, potential investors and customers, even current and potential employees. The premium positioning of a firm in terms of pricing potential and reputation associated with a viable *unique competing space* has been addressed earlier in this chapter. A growth company commands a premium position in other ways; this might be expressed, for example, in terms of price–earnings multiples based on future profitability potential. Alternatively, it might simply be the immense psychological boost to employees and other key stakeholders derived from being associated with a "hot" company, and the excitement of being part of that momentum. Facebook and Twitter, it is said, have attracted a lot of engineering talent from formerly "hot" technology companies such as Google and Microsoft. Companies that continually challenge their *value proposition* and nurture their *unique competing space* never acquire the staleness that befalls companies who lose their competitive position in the market place.

We have argued that the firm's *value proposition* provides the substantiation of its *unique competing space*. An important implication of this is that it is exclusively within the domain of the firm's *unique competing space* that we would expect to find viable strategic options. We explore the relevance of the firm's *unique competing space* in the context of strategic options more closely in Chapter 7.

Importantly, the firm's *unique competing space* is not a stagnant domain. It represents a dynamic domain that is continually subjected to perturbations at its boundaries as competitive circumstances change. Changing conditions at the firm's strategic boundaries might relate to threats to its existing competitive position as much as they might represent new opportunities for growth. Changing competitive conditions can be readily visualized with the help of the *unique competing space* framework. Imagine the scenario mapped in Figure 5.3:

1. Changes are occurring in the external macro-environment; these might be driven by changes in the firm's macro-economic, regulatory, technological and/or socio-economic environment. Changes in the macro-economic environment have a trickle-down effect that leads to changes in the firm's industry context, and, ultimately, in the markets in which it is competing.

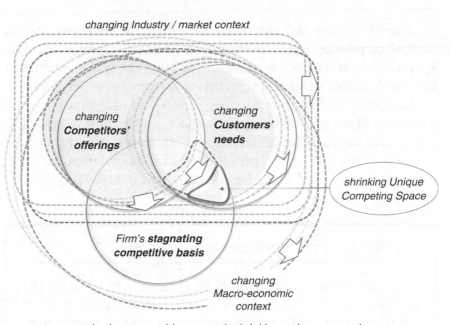

Figure 5.3 Losing competitive ground: shrinking unique competing space

2. Customers' needs are changing, reflecting changes in the firm's market space; entirely new market opportunities might be emerging. Changes in the "customer" domain may also include changing stakeholder positions.
3. Competitors are threatening the firm's unique competitive position; in fact, they are encroaching on the firm's competitive space. Competitor pressure may reflect increasing strength of existing competitors, the emergence of new entrants to the market, or substitutions to the extant market offering.
4. Critically, the firm has not held its competitive ground. It has not responded appropriately to changes in its competitive environment and it has failed to successfully fend off competitors' encroachment of its unique competing space. This has resulted in loss of competitive ground.

Loss of competitive ground is shown by the shrinking unique competitive space. The firm's position of competitive advantage is thereby seriously compromised and as a consequence its unique competing space is shrinking. What has happened? The spatial perspective of the unique competing space enables a powerful means of examining this question by an exploration of the firm's strategic boundaries – the boundaries that form the periphery of its unique competing space. In the next section we will examine the firm's strategic boundaries, the impact of changes to the conditions prevailing at the boundaries and strategic implications of these for the firm's competitive position.

Box 5.3 BlackBerry Crushed

Not that long ago the BlackBerry smartphone was the premier mobile gadget and a genuine tech status symbol. As recently as 2009 the Blackberry's parent company RIM was named by FORTUNE to be one of the fastest growing companies in the world, with earnings growing by 84% a year. No longer. Multiple missteps have seen its market share plummet from 50% in 2007 to just over 11% in July 2012 as customers are dropping the once ubiquitous smartphone for *Apple iPhones* and *Google Android* devices. Numerous reasons exist for the difficulties RIM's Black-Berry is experiencing, of course. However, on the basis of insights offered by sources close to the embattled smartphone maker these might be broadly grouped into three main clusters representing the intersecting circles of RIM's *unique competing space,* beginning with the lower circle representing RIM's internal competitive basis:

1. *Embattled internal turf:* One of the key disabling forces cited in explaining RIM's recent difficulties is the split personality in the executive suite. While one of the CEOs, company founder Mike Lazardis, was pushing for a make-or-break launch of a next-generation BlackBerry with a new operating system, his co-CEO Jim Basille, was intensifying efforts on a separate strategy focused on licensing some of the company's proprietary technology.

Compounding this problem, and arguably at the root of RIM's current dilemma, has been a blinding confidence in the basic BlackBerry. With both executives now gone, it remains to be seen whether the new CEO, former Lazaridis lieutenant Thorsten Heins, will succeed in steering the troubled company clear of its difficulties.

2. *Disunity over who the customer really is:* Related to the internal conflict has been a prolonged debate over RIM's core customers; that is, who these really are. Not only has this added to the internal tensions, but it has led to a series of unsuccessful catch-up products that fell short of generating the intended market impact. RIM ultimately failed to anticipate that private consumers and not business customers were driving the evolution of the smartphone market. RIM's perception of smartphone customer's needs revolved around e-mail functionality. It realized only too late that the market had moved on; the BlackBerry's e-mail functionality (which, notably, experienced several widespread blackouts in 2011) no longer excited smartphone customers.

3. *Formidable competitors' offerings.* More fundamentally, however, RIM has failed to respond to the emerging applications (apps) economy. This has endowed its competitors, *Apple's iPhone* and a multitude of *Android* devices, with a devastating advantage. While it was yet preoccupied with e-mail functionality, RIM's competitors envisioned entirely new modes of connected communication consisting of powerful mobile computers that provided not only e-mail services but also enabled Web-browsing on the go. They also introduced "next-wave" mechanisms that supported mass adoption of their products and services, such as platforms for developers to create applications that embedded user experience.

Sources: 1. Connors, W. (2012) Multiple Missteps Caused Research in Motion's Fall, *Wall Street Journal* (2 July 2012); 2. Gustin, S. (2012) Blackberry Crushed, *TIME* (16 July 2012).

STRATEGY IN PRACTICE: SHRINKING COMPETITION POSITIONS

Companies typically find themselves in situations in which their unique competing space is shrinking when:

- . . . they fail to observe shifts in their external competitive environment; continue to compete in ways that may previously have offered potential for competitive differentiation but now no longer provide the basis for competitive advantage.
- . . . they fail to protect their unique competing space against encroaching competitors. This may happen when companies fail to recognize new competition; when they fail to protect their assets – or, simply when they fail to sustain their competitive edge through neglect of their strategically relevant resources and capabilities.
- . . . they lose touch with their customers and fail to understand their customers' changing needs.

Strategic Boundaries of the Unique Competing Space

Figure 5.2 suggests that the firm's *unique competing space* is a domain bounded by three interfaces. The three interfaces form the boundaries of the firm's unique competing space. Each boundary carries different strategic implications for the firm's competitive position. Viewed collectively, the three boundaries provide a powerful perspective on the firm's competitive position. The first boundary (indicated by "1" in Figure 5.4) represents the interface to the firm's competitors. The boundary labeled "2" represents the interface of the firm to its customers. The third strategic boundary, labeled "3" in Figure 5.4, represents a firm–internal interface or threshold across which the firm must transfer capabilities and resources relevant to the unique opportunity presented by the customers' needs.

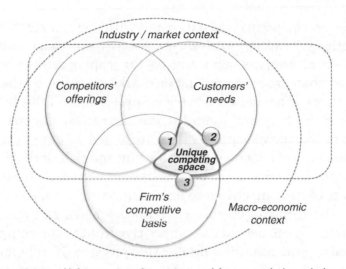

Figure 5.4   Unique competing space and its strategic boundaries

Let's examine each of the three strategic boundaries and their implications in turn.

"The Line of Demarcation": Strategic Boundary "1"

The strategic boundary designated as "*1*" (Figure 5.4) represents a line of demarcation; the competitive front facing the firm's competitors and their offerings. Notably, competitors along this front are also in a position to deliver a value offering that addresses needs of the customers in the market segment in question to a limited extent. This common ground domain is represented by the triangular space formed by the intersection of all three circles; it is a hotly contested field of competition in which the firm and all its competitors are in a position to deliver a value offering that *partially* fulfills the market's needs. The firm's *unique competing space*, on the other hand, represents that opportunity space in which the firm (ideally) alone is in a position to create and deliver value in a way that its competitors cannot. Note that in reality, the firm may actually share its "unique" competing space with one or a few other competitors. The salient point, however, is that the firm's *unique competing space* represents an opportunity that is *strategically attractive*, even if shared with one or a very few other competitors. By *strategically attractive* we mean that competition in this space presents opportunities for reaping returns on effort invested that exceed comparable market returns of the firm's competitors. What are the strategic implications of this boundary for the firm? First and foremost the firm must understand the nature of the "demarcation", the nature and extent of the differentiation between its own value offering and that of the competitors'. Second, the firm must protect its competitive turf against any attempts of its competitors to encroach on its *unique competing space*. The firm can do this via both defensive and preemptive approaches. It can defend its competitive front to the competition by suitable protection of its intellectual property (IP) inherent to its unique value offering; this might include patents, copyright and trademarks. Furthermore, it can invest in preemptive measures that strengthen and consolidate the advantage represented by its *unique competing space*; this might include strategic investments in building its brand. Another powerful, likewise preemptive, measure would be to invest effort in building and nurturing the firm's innovation capabilities. Innovating faster than the competition is a most effective mechanism for protecting the firm's *unique competing space* from competitors' threatening advances.

BOX 5.4 NEWCOMERS ON THE BLOCK

The small but growing market for niche, boutique ski makers in the USA is an example of how a number of small companies are drawing new lines of demarcation in a relatively mature market space. Currently, some 80 niche ski makers, mostly in snowy states like Maine and Wyoming, are going face to face with big-name ski manufacturers, including *Fischer*, *K2*, *Dynastar* and *Völkl* – who still control 90% of the USD 533 million ski market, but who are relying increasingly on manufacturing of their skis in overseas locations, with about 35% of their skis currently made in China.

Chinese-manufactured skis no longer cut it for a growing segment of older, diehard and affluent skiers who tend to have time and money to ski often. Increasingly, these skiers are gravitating to hand-crafted, high-tech and high-end skis that satisfy specific experiences like deep-powder skiing in a way that Chinese-made skis cannot. The boutique ski makers who specialize in making hand-crafted skis, often out of a living room, garage and local machine shop rather than a foreign factory, are meeting the demands of the emerging ski segment. They have been described as "small companies that bring a huge amount of passion and innovation to the industry . . . they're going up against the Goliaths, but they have very specific target markets and are selling to very specific customers . . . ". The competitive prospects of the boutique ski makers are promising; they generated between USD 20 million and 30 million per year through the economic downturn and are set to capture another 3 to 5% of the ski markets in the next 5 to 10 years according to industry experts. At prices up to USD 2,300 for a custom-milled pair of skis and yearly sales growth as high as 80%, the newcomers on the block are indeed a group to be watched.

Source: Diddlebock, B. (2012) Sweet Spot. Niche Skimakers are Making a Run for Diehard Skiers, *TIME Europe Edition* (9 April 2012).

"The Customer Interface": Strategic Boundary "2"

The importance of nurturing an intimate relationship with one's customers is undisputed. The unique competing space framework provides a graphical perspective of what this implies in the greater competitive context. The boundary designated "2" in Figure 5.4 represents the firm's interface to its customers and markets. In a broader sense, this includes the firm's community of stakeholders. This boundary is strategically relevant because it represents the interface across which the firm ultimately delivers its unique value offering to its stakeholders. The better the firm understands and "manages" this interface, the better its ability to ensure delivery of its value offering across this boundary. Strategic management of this interface requires an understanding of the customers' needs that in cases may exceed the market's own understanding of its needs. Firms might use emerging techniques such as ethnography and advanced customer relationship management approaches to achieve this understanding. Needless to point out, understanding and insights developed at the customer interface provide important impulses for appropriate measures directed at boundary "1". This might include unique insights that might trigger new, innovative forms of the value offering to address emerging needs in the market.

Successful firms deal with their customer interface in different ways. Amazon.com CEO and founder Jeff Bezos' quirky habit of using an empty chair to symbolize the customer at Amazon's strategy meetings is an example from someone who has been touted as one of America's best-performing CEOs.[5]

"The Internal Threshold": Strategic Boundary "3"

Of the three boundaries, the internal threshold is the least obvious and, arguably, the most critical to the firm's ability to build and sustain its competitiveness. From a *resource-based* perspective, the lower circle depicting the firm's competitive basis represents its repository of resources and capabilities. However, mere possession of resources and capabilities does not endow the firm with any competitive advantage. The firm's resources and capabilities must be configured in a way that they are relevant to the firm's unique competing space – and figuratively transferred across the boundary "3" to be of any strategic relevance. The firm's stock of resources and capabilities, encompassing both tangible and intangible forms, are embedded in an organizational context that consists of the organization's processes, structure, culture, practices and mechanisms – and ultimately, leadership. Strategic utilization of the firm's resources requires astute and skillful orchestration of the entire organizational context. In terms of the five building blocks of strategy introduced in Chapter 1 (Box 1.2), interface "*3*" addresses the fifth building block, which is about "getting the organizational act together".

Not all of the firm's resources are equally relevant or appropriate for creating the value offering that underpins its *unique competing space*. Some of the firm's resources may, in fact, be outdated and therefore no longer of strategic relevance for any of the firm's value offerings. Moreover, a firm's organizational context might be averse to creating value; its culture, processes and practices may not be optimally aligned for exploiting its resources and capabilities in accordance with the value that is to be created. In this sense strategic boundary "*3*" represents an internal organizational *threshold* across which relevant resources and capabilities need to be configured and mobilized in order for that value on the basis of which the firm aspires to stake its competitive claim to be created. Boundary "*3*" lies clearly within the perimeter of the circle representing the firm's basis of competitiveness. This carries important implications: mobilization of the firm's resources and capabilities across this threshold boundary are entirely within the firm's sphere of control.

Resources that are relevant to the firm's *unique competing space* must be appropriately bundled, configured and mobilized across the internal threshold (boundary "*3*") in order to be of any competitive relevance to the firm. Many firms fail to achieve this. Despite claiming ownership of resources that are potentially relevant to their *unique competing space*, they do not succeed in mobilizing them across the internal threshold.

Why does this happen? There are many possible reasons. Firms sometimes are not fully aware of what they possess in terms of potential strategic resources and capabilities. Firms often "*don't know what they know*" and consequently fail to exploit their own strategic resources. Or, firms simply don't succeed in "getting their act together"; aligning their resources, processes, practices and culture in ways that allow them to fully exploit their strategic potential in changing markets. Cases of lost opportunity of this type abound. Eastman Kodak is a case in point: the venerable manufacturer of traditional silver halide roll-film has seen its markets collapse over the past decade. A combination of structural and cultural hurdles has prevented the group's ability to change quickly enough, forcing the Kodak to file for Chapter 11 bankruptcy protection in January 2012.

Inter-Relationships Between Boundaries and Strategic Boundary Conditions

Each of the three boundaries is important in its own way, but there are important linkages between the boundaries. Improved understanding derived from insight into customers' needs (boundary "2" in Figure 5.4) is relevant to both of the other boundaries. Each of the other two boundaries is affected by its complementary boundaries in a similar manner. Competitively successful firms preemptively orchestrate activities at all three boundaries in response to changing conditions as they evolve. It is when firms fail to do this that their unique competing space is threatened.

The notion of a strategic *boundary condition* is borrowed from the physical sciences where boundary conditions define the nature of a domain at its periphery. From the physical sciences analogy we also understand that changes to the domain are typically initiated through perturbations at its boundaries. Perturbations at its periphery characteristically provide first indications of an impending change to the prevailing situation within the domain. Weather fronts are a case in point; minor disturbances that develop into major changes to the prevailing weather system are discernible initially at the system's periphery.

And so it is with competitive business environments. These are also complex, riddled with ambiguity and continually changing. Complexity in business environments stems from the fact that multiple factors are at play at any point in time. This leads to changing conditions in the firm's competitive environment. Firms characteristically experience this initially as disturbances to conditions at the boundaries of their competing space. Because these often act on more than one boundary, the sum effect may be complex.

Changing conditions at boundary "*1*" may result when existing or new competitors appear on the scene with an improved value offering that appeals to customers' needs. Expiring intellectual property protection may represent another change at the line of demarcation to the firm's competitors. Changes to conditions at boundary "*2*" may reflect changing customer tastes and prefer- ences – triggered possibly by new offerings introduced to the market by competitors. Alternatively, they might reflect chang- ing stakeholder needs and positions of power to influence deci- sion making. Finally, change to the firm's internal threshold (boundary "*3*") may result when firms excessively cut investment in their R&D, become complacent in nurturing new capabilities and fall prey to organizational inertia.

Most firms can cope with change at one of its boundaries. The situation becomes more critical when firms experience signifi- cant change at two of its boundaries simultaneously. Many firms end up in a competitive tailspin when facing substantial change at all three of their boundaries at the same time.

Changing Boundary Conditions and Strategic Sense Making

Changing conditions at the firm's strategic boundaries compel the firm to engage in sense making. Perturbations at the firm's strategic boundaries give rise to critical issues that prompt the need for sense making in the first place. The strategic boundary perspective provides a profoundly useful means of "cutting to the chase" of the strategic matter at hand. Strategic issues, when they arise, invariably do so when the firm experiences perturbations at one or more of its strategic boundaries. Even changes seemingly far removed from the immediate firm context, such as changes in the firm's macro-economic environment, can trigger trickle-down effects resulting in changes in the industry and market environments that are of immediate relevance to the firm. The impact of these changes, if strategically relevant to the firm's competitive position, will have an impact on one or more of the boundaries of its unique competing space.

The focus on the firm's strategic boundaries when seeking to make sense of strategic challenges – regardless of whether prompted by threats or opportunities – enables a considerable narrowing of the focus on issues that are, indeed, strategically relevant from the outset. This has important implications for the quality of the sense making: first, it enables firms to focus and concentrate relatively quickly on the essence of the relevant strategic challenge. Time can be a critical factor when firms need to make sense of factors underlying emerging strategic challenges. The ability to "cut to the chase" on strategic issues quickly can be an immense competitive advantage. Second, the ability to focus on the essence of a strategic matter from the outset helps firms from getting distracted by issues that are irrelevant to the challenge at hand. Finally, an analysis that quickly converges on the core of the strategic problem at stake enables precision and rigor in the articulation of the strategic questions to be addressed and resolved.

Invariably, changing conditions seldom affect only one of the boundaries. This increases the complexity of the analysis in that a purely rational approach is seldom adequate. Sense making must draw on a combination of inputs; insights based on informed intuition, a continual challenging of assumptions and realistic interpretation of multiple signals through rational analysis.

When engaging in strategic sense making many managers often find themselves randomly searching for the proverbial "needle in the haystack" when it comes to framing issues and articulating strategically relevant questions. Too often, this approach amounts to little more than "shooting at clay pigeons with a shotgun in the dark". Probability would have it that one might occasionally actually hit a clay pigeon; more often than not, however, the effort remains futile. The *unique competing space*, in particular, a focused analysis of its boundary conditions, provides a profoundly more powerful approach to the task.

Unique Competing Space: A Portfolio Perspective

A firm's competitive position is typically based on a *portfolio* of individual value offerings that are substantiated by respective unique and superior value propositions. Individual value offerings are each represented by respective unique competing spaces. A *unique competing space* (and by extension, *value proposition*) can be defined for any value offering for which it is possible to define: (1) a specific customer/stakeholder need to be fulfilled; (2) a disposition, ability and capacity on the part of the firm to fulfill that need – ideally, in a uniquely superior way; and (3) potential competitors. Hence, one can envisage the firm consisting of a portfolio of unique competing spaces (Figure 5.5). Individual unique competing spaces in that portfolio will invariably exhibit differing degrees of competitive impact; this will be reflected by their size. Some might be

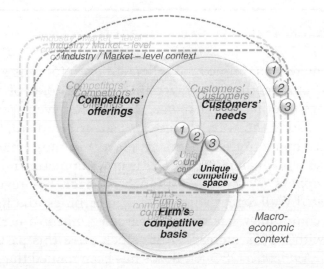

Figure 5.5   Unique competing space: portfolio perspective

relatively small – such as in emerging or maturing markets, while relatively few might contribute a disproportionate share of the impact. One can think of this in terms of the *Pareto principle*, whereby, for example, 80% of the firm's competitive impact is derived from 20% of the firm's value offerings. It is the collective competitive impact of the firm's portfolio of unique competing spaces that is at stake. This determines the firm's overall position of competitiveness. The firm's strategic objective is, therefore, to optimize the strategic impact of its portfolio of unique competing spaces over all of its value offerings. This can be a daunting task when considering that the average Global 1000 company competes in approximately 52 markets.

It is important to note that the depiction of the firm's portfolio of *unique competing spaces* as circles of equal size represents an idealization. In practice it is highly unlikely that the firm's portfolio of unique competing spaces will be comprised of domains of equal magnitude. Strategic management of the firm's portfolio of unique competing spaces demands maximization of its position across its entire portfolio of value offerings. This invariably amounts to a complex and multi-dimensional challenge.

BOX 5.5 AMAZONIAN VALUE DISRUPTOR

Once merely an online bookseller, *Amazon* today is a $100 billion empire that has diversified its portfolio of value offerings to other merchandise, devices and even web services. Along the way, the internet giant has disruptively upended many of the incumbent players in those markets. Its recently launched *Kindle Fire* is now competing head-on with *Apple's iPad Mini*. Although Amazon has regularly frustrated Wall Street with its erratic earnings, the investment community has richly rewarded *Amazon's* performance with a 30% increase in its stock price this past year (2012). *Amazon's* CEO Jeff Bezos has been named the *FORTUNE 2012 "Businessperson of the Year"*.

Much of *Amazon's* success, arguably, can be traced to what Bezos frequently refers to as the *"the three big ideas at Amazon"*: (1) long-term thinking, (2) customer obsession, and (3) a willingness to invent. Collectively these three credos distinguish and define *Amazon's "unique competing space"*. Individually, each of the "ideas" can be readily mapped to one of the three boundaries encompassing its *UCS*.

Amazon's long-term thinking credo manifests itself in several ways: at its core is an astute understanding of the competition – and its differentiated position relative to these. The internet giant has always taken the long-term view – and has habitually ignored Wall Street's pleas for consistent earnings growth. On the other hand, it has clearly set itself apart from its Silicon Valley counterparts, including *Apple*, who pride themselves on their ability to sell high-profit devices that generate premium margins. *Amazon* has always sold low- or no-profit devices at the bare minimum required to break even – in favour of ever more volume. One of Bezos's favourite sayings is: *"Your margin is my opportunity"*.

Even as *Amazon's* portfolio of market offerings has expanded, it has zealously maintained focus on delivering a good *customer experience* across its multiple market interfaces. *Amazon's* customer experience credo is closely coupled to its obsession with the last of its three credos: its organizational capability in *innovation*. Both are deeply embedded in the company's culture. Bezos on how the two are linked: *"We innovate by starting with the customer and working backwards. That becomes the touchstone for how we invent"*. Moreover, this forms the basis of *Amazon's* differentiated strategic stance – as Bezos explains: *"When they're [the competition] in the shower in the morning, they're thinking about how they're going to get ahead of one of their top competitors. Here in the shower, we're thinking about how we are going to invent something on behalf of a customer"*.

High margin – focused competitors are well advised to heed *Amazon's* understated disruptive threat, succinctly articulated by Bezos: *"Other companies have more of a conqueror mentality; we think of ourselves as explorers"*.

Source: Lashinsky, A. (2012) Jeff Bezos: The Ultimate Disruptor, *FORTUNE Europe Edition* (3 December 2012)

Summary and Limitations

The power of the *unique competing space* framework derives from the comprehensiveness and the incisiveness it contributes to the strategic analysis on a high level. Similar to the *value proposition* framework, it assembles and integrates factors related to a firm's external and internal competitive positions in the context of its strategic mandate. The *unique competing space* presents a graphical depiction of the firm's competitive window of opportunity; it provides a mapping of the firm's strategic landscape.

As with all abstractions of reality, there are caveats worth noting when applying the *unique competing space* framework. The Venn diagram depiction of the firm's competitive position is deceptively simple; it is a simplification of reality. In reality, the boundaries demarcating competitors might be far from obvious; markets might be emerging and difficult to identify on the radar screen. Figure 5.2 portrays the circles representing competitors, customers/markets and the firm to be of equal diameter. This is unlikely to be the case in reality; the exact size and borders of the three elements might be difficult to discern; this might be further compounded by perturbations at the peripheries of the unique competing space which blur actual happenings at the individual boundaries. The two-dimensional depiction of the *unique competing space* in Figure 5.2 is another abstraction; firms' competitive environments are typically multidimensional with windows of competitive opportunities existing in adjacent markets and contiguous competitors. This is difficult to depict in two dimensions.

Limitations aside, the *unique competing space* can be profoundly useful in guiding our strategic thinking in a way that enables us to focus on the essence of the strategic matter at hand without losing sight of the greater competitive context in question.

STRATEGY IN PRACTICE: CRITICAL REFLECTION ON YOUR FIRM'S UNIQUE COMPETING SPACE . . .

- What's the unique value at its core?
- What makes it unique and superior?
- What makes it most vulnerable – and why so?
- How clearly discernible are the boundaries of your firm's competing space?
- If not clearly discernible, why might this be the case?
- Which of the boundaries is most critical to your firm's position of competitive advantage – and why so?
- What are the critical issues at the critical boundaries – and why?
- What issues might be the result of compounded effects of simultaneous perturbations at several boundaries?

Opportunity–Response (O–R) Analysis Framework

The *opportunity–response* framework, which is examined in the final section of this chapter, probes both external and internal perspectives. This framework contributes insights that link relevant external and internal contexts, but it does not explicitly relate these to the strategic value issue at stake. This is the key difference between high-level frameworks discussed earlier in this chapter and the opportunity-response framework of analysis. This framework does, however, probe the final important strategic question – the *"when?"* question, which is addressed by neither the *value proposition* nor the *unique competing space* frameworks. The *opportunity–response* framework brings both external and internal perspectives into juxtaposition and introduces a time perspective to the analysis.

The *opportunity–response* analysis framework brings together a number of elements of strategic analysis that collectively yield potentially useful insights. The framework presented in Figure 5.6 consists of two axes representing a time horizon (horizontal axis) and a vertical axis representing an appropriate performance measure (for example, market share growth, or a return on investment), and two intersecting curves. The upper curve (labeled *"1"*), depicted by a decreasing function, represents *market opportunity* as it evolves in the company's external competitive environment. The lower curve (labeled *"2"*) depicted by an increasing function represents the *firm's*

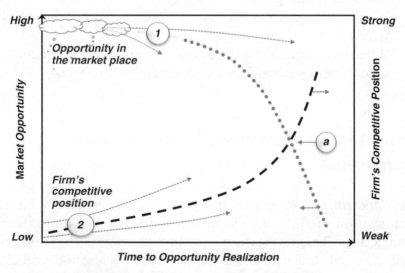

Figure 5.6 *Opportunity–response* framework

response to that market opportunity. More precisely, curve *"2"* reflects the firm's competitive position relative to the market opportunity at any point along the time horizon. The firm's competitive position is an indication of its ability to deliver on the market opportunity represented by the upper curve (labeled *"1"*).

As such, the lower curve (*"1"*) in Figure 5.7 captures the firm's internal basis of competitiveness; its knowledge, capabilities, resources and organizational wherewithal relative to the market opportunity at any point in time. The lower curve is therefore sometimes referred to as the company's *knowledge* or *experience* curve. At some point in time, the firm's ability to respond to a market opportunity matches the specific demands of that opportunity. This point is depicted by the intersection of the two curves at the point labeled *"a"*. The *opportunity–response* framework thus addresses a final question in addition to the *where, how, why* and *what* questions posed in conjunction with the value proposition framework. It introduces the *"when?"* question to the strategic equation to be resolved. The opportunity–response analysis suggests that the timing of a firm's response is not arbitrary; that it is dependent on the firm's ability to position itself appropriate to the market opportunity in order to successfully exploit that opportunity.

The graphical form of the approach represented by the opportunity–response framework appears to have been first proposed by DeGenaro[6] in 1991. We will see further on, however, that the framework's underpinning rationale has its strategy roots in a framework proposed by Andrews[7] in 1971. The schematic is essentially a graphical representation of the simple *SWOT* (*strengths, weaknesses, opportunities, threats*) framework. The upper curve, shown in Figure 5.7 as *"1"*, represents opportunities and/or threats in the firm's external competitive context. The lower curve (*"2"*) represents the firm's strengths and/or weaknesses that relate to its internal basis of competitiveness.

STRATEGY IN PRACTICE: THE *SWOT* ANALYSIS

The origins of the *SWOT* (acronym for *strengths, weaknesses, opportunities, threats*) analysis are not entirely clear; it is known to have been used by Harvard Business School academics in the late 1960s. Despite its popularity with managers, the analysis does not have any basis in theory as such; indeed, it has even been suggested that its origins may be tied to an idea sketched out by a professor on the back of an envelope one day – that just caught on. The attractiveness of the *SWOT* may lie in its beguiling simplicity. However, therein also lie its limitations. There are several critical ones:

- First, the *SWOT* is outdated. Our understanding of real business contexts has evolved since the *SWOT* appeared on the scene. We now appreciate that strategy in complex contexts rarely allows a black and white approach to sense making suggested by the *SWOT*. In practice, strategy often demands *trade-offs*; *SWOT* does not deal with these well.
- Second, the *SWOT* is inherently imprecise. For example, it does little to help delineate the strategic impact of the firm's resources. It does not discriminate between strategic resources – such as the firm's core capabilities – and those of an enabling or supporting type. Neither does the SWOT support the strategic analysis of emerging assets, such as new, emerging technologies.
- Most critical, however, is the potential ambiguity introduced by the *SWOT*. A case in point: consider, for example, the combination of a highly skilled labor force coupled with stable labor relations typically found in German companies. Is this a "strength" or a "weakness" for German companies? We might be initially inclined to identify this as a "strength". However, when facing the need to react quickly to changing market conditions demanding headcount flexibility, this apparent strength can quickly

become a restricting liability in view of Germany's rigid labor laws that constrain rapid headcount reduction. So, the best insight a *SWOT* can muster on this potentially critical issue is an enigmatic *"it depends"*.

- As with other inherently "scattergun" approaches, the *SWOT* analysis provides little guidance to managers on suitable next steps.

The point is that while there is nothing inherently *wrong* with the *SWOT* analysis, managers have significantly better approaches to fall back on. Profoundly more insightful approaches, such as the *value proposition* and *unique competing space* frameworks examined in the previous chapter, include elements of analysis touched by the *SWOT*, but they take the sense making analysis significantly further – while, importantly, retaining the focus on the essence of the strategic challenge at stake.

Source: Haberberg (2000).[8]

Opportunity–Response: Competing Trajectories

Clearly, the depiction of a firm's competitive position relative to opportunities in its competitive environment in Figure 5.7 is a simplification of reality. In reality, we would expect to find multiple trajectories emerging from a "cloud" of potential opportunities on the market opportunity side. Some of these opportunities dissipate and disappear rather quickly. Other trajectories, of course, materialize as viable market opportunities, although often this is apparent only retrospectively since trajectories representing market opportunities are typically difficult to discern when they first appear.

Market opportunities are triggered by environments that are in flux, driven by multiple drivers such as changing consumer needs, emerging technologies and/or competitor activity. Opportunities emerging as a result of disruptive innovation might initially exist in competing forms that ultimately give way to a dominant form of the technology in question. New market opportunities emerge and exist for both incumbents and new entrants, though the inherent risk is often greater for the incumbent.[9,10] Often, what appears to be an opportunity for a new entrant or challenger represents a threat to the incumbent.

Some apparent opportunities are delayed in their realization and ultimately don't materialize in the way originally anticipated. An example is the *UMTS (Universal Mobile Telecommunications Systems)* third generation (*3G*) telecommunications licensing drive in 2000. UMTS, the third generation mobile cellular technology for networks based on the GSM standard, was viewed by telecommunication players as the coming network platform. The auctioning of the licenses unleashed a bidding frenzy between telecommunications providers at the height of the dotcom boom. Mobile operators around the world, though mainly in Europe, ended up paying a total of $125 billion for licenses to build and operate *3G* networks that ultimately failed to materialize in the way originally anticipated.

On the firm response side, we would similarly expect to find multiple competing trajectories representing competing firms vying to capture the same opportunity. Not all of the competitors will necessarily be starting from the same competitive position due to the unique legacies and path dependencies of the competing firms. Differences in starting points reflect asymmetries in the competitive positions of the competitors eyeing the same market opportunities. The rate of acceleration of individual competitors along their respective learning trajectory is determined by the competitive agility of the firms. Some competitors invariably drop out along the way.

Opportunity-Side Perspective

Market-side thinking in the late 1960s and 1970s was largely influenced by attempts to make sense of markets through analyses of the external competitive context. Porter's[11] *structure–conduct–performance* paradigm with roots in industrial–organizational economics represented a breakthrough in *opportunity-side* thinking when it was introduced in the late 1970s. It was to dominate strategic thinking in the 1970s and much of the 1980s. The structure–conduct–performance paradigm confined the firm's strategic role to scrutinizing and scanning the external competitive environment for opportunities and threats – and to orienting the firm's strategic course on this basis accordingly. The premise of the structure–conduct–performance paradigm was that while the external context cannot be influenced by any individual firm, firms must nonetheless understand their competitive environment and "adjust" their internal basis of competitiveness accordingly. However, little if any guidance on what this "adjusting" might entail, or how firms were to go about it was available at the time.

Response-Side Perspective

Response-side thinking emerged in the 1990s with the development of the *resource-based view* (RBV) of the firm.[12–14] The premise of the resource-based view is that a firm's basis of competitive advantage derives from its ability and capacity to configure and exploit its resources and capabilities in a uniquely superior way. Strategic competences, capabilities and the embedded knowledge and learning, and the organization's ability to configure these in ways that enable the firm to create uniquely differentiated value offerings, are at the core of the organization's competitiveness. Notably, these activities are entirely within the firm's own sphere of control and disposition. The resource-based view thereby shifted the strategic emphasis from the external environment to the company's internal context; its ability to respond appropriately to opportunity in the external environment. An important point to be noted: the curve depicting the organization's learning trajectory as a smooth curve is a substantial simplification of what we might expect to find in reality. A firm's learning (or experience) trajectory may exhibit critical discontinuities and even disruptive setbacks. Another factor not suggested by the smooth curves representing competitors' trajectories is that there might be interactions between the curves, such as collusion, possibly even cooperation related to some form of strategic partnering between some of the competitors.

Opportunity–Response: A Dynamic Capabilities Perspective

The *opportunity–response* framework aligns the external competitive environment and the organization's internal basis of competitiveness and presents these in a dynamic context that is continually in flux. External contexts in which opportunities originate are more often than not complex, ambiguous and defy any attempts at rational sense making. The firm's response under these circumstances necessitates a dynamic predisposition and ability on the part of the firm. Recent thinking in the management literature focused on the notion of *dynamic capabilities* has suggested new approaches to the task. While there is yet little consensus among strategy scholars on the exact nature of dynamics, there is nonetheless general agreement that dynamic capabilities encompass the disposition, capacity and ability of a firm to respond appropriately to a need or opportunity for change.[15–17]

In positioning the role of dynamic capabilities in this context it has been argued that it is not so much the positions companies occupy in an industry landscape as it is what they *do*; how they take cues from opportunities arising in their environment, how they reconfigure their own ideas and capabilities to develop new innovative value offerings and how they then deliver these to the market.[9] However, resources and capabilities do not effortlessly combine and reconfigure to form new capabilities. *Dynamic capabilities* are thought to play a key role in this activity that leads to the renewal and strategic repositioning of the firm. Dynamic capabilities are defined as *"the ability to sense and then seize new opportunities, and to reconfigure and protect*

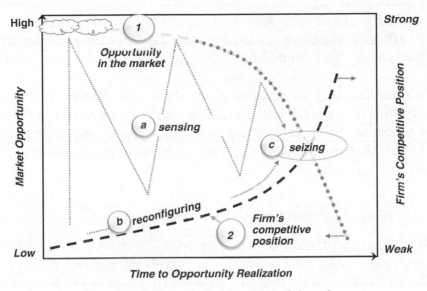

Figure 5.7 Opportunity–response and dynamic

knowledge assets, competencies and complementary assets so as to achieve sustained competitive advantage".[9]

Figure 5.7 positions the three activities suggested by Teece's[9] notion of dynamic capabilities schematically in the context of the *opportunity–response* framework.

Each of the three activities leading up to and including the seizing of the respective market opportunity can be considered to represent a class of dynamic capability. The first activity, *sensing* (denoted by *"a"*) is essentially a detecting and sense making activity that focuses on identifying and correctly assessing opportunity trajectories as they emerge in the external environment of the firm. On the basis of the market insight that emerges from this activity, resources and capabilities within are *reconfigured* (denoted by *"b"*) in alignment with the interpretation of the market opportunity. The sensing and reconfiguring activities occur progressively over numerous cycles as the competitive position of the firm evolves to match the market opportunity. Finally, when resources and capabilities have been appropriately reconfigured to match the opportunity, the company exploits and captures the opportunity through *seizing* (denoted by *"c"*).

Despite the lack of agreement on the exact role of dynamic capabilities in the reconfiguration of resources, one can nonetheless conclude that this critical strategic task cannot be left to chance; that it demands deliberate, purposeful and entrepreneurial management effort.

Matching Opportunity with Response

The *opportunity–response* framework prompts us to think about the match between what an organization *might* do given opportunities and threats that present themselves in the firm's competitive environment and what it *can* do at any point in time given its organizational strengths and vulnerabilities. The underlying concept has actually been around for some time. Andrews, in his classic book *The Concept of Corporate Strategy*,[7] defined strategy as the match between what the firm *might* do given the opportunities in its competitive environment and what the firm *can* do on the basis of its internal basis of competitiveness as early as 1971.

The manner in which firms approach competitive repositioning in view of emerging market opportunities is critical to their competitiveness. While there is no standard approach, the schematic in Figure 5.8 does suggest a generic algorithm that draws on the thinking of both Andrews[7] and Grant.[13] It shows how the activity focused on matching resources and capabilities to opportunities in the environment might be carried out in practice. The schematic suggests another important point; it underscores a key conceptual difference between the *structure–conduct–performance* approach to strategy of the 1970s and 1980s and the *resource-based view* introduced in the 1990s. The scheme suggests how a firm might proceed in crafting a deliberate and purposeful response on the basis of an assessment

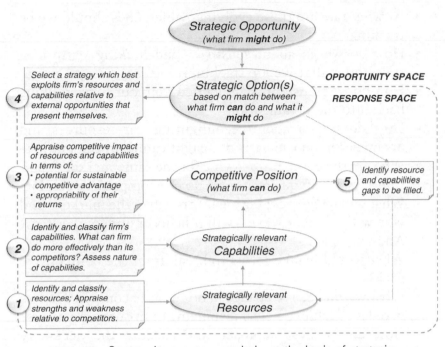

Figure 5.8 Opportunity–response analysis on the basis of strategic opportunity assessment

of its resources and capabilities.[18] Capabilities as a manifestation of organizational knowledge are dependent on learning for their development. However one defines resources and capabilities, the objective of the assessment is to match what the company *might* do on the basis of the opportunities in the environment, and what it currently *can* do as a result of its resource and capability position.

STRATEGY IN PRACTICE: QUESTIONS PROMPTED BY THE *OPPORTUNITY–RESPONSE* ANALYSIS

- What are the underlying drivers and trends that are shaping the trajectories representing market opportunities in our competitive environment?

- At what rate are these evolving; which ones should we be tracking?
- How do we go about *sensing* – and *making sense of* – trajectories that we are tracking?
- How do we transfer insight gained from our *sense making* back into the organization?
- How do we go about reconfiguring our resources and organization on the basis of insight gained in the market?
- Who are the competitors vying for the same market opportunity; what unique attributes do our competitors exhibit?
- What will be the next big breakthrough in the market – and who will ride that wave – will it be us or our competitors? And why so?
- What would it take for us to break from the competitive pack?
- What would need to change in our basis of competitiveness in order to achieve a clear distancing from our competitors?
- How do we best approach and execute the necessary acceleration of our learning trajectory?

SUMMARIZING THE CHAPTER . . .

- High-level frameworks of analysis focus sense making and strategic analysis on the "big picture" by probing both the firm's external and internal environments in the context of its strategic mandate – that of creating and delivering a differentiated value offering.
- The purpose of high-level analysis is to guide the overall strategic thinking and sense making; to help not "lose sight of the wood for the trees".
- The two high-level frameworks examined – the *value proposition* and *unique competing space* frameworks – probe the *"where"*, *"why"*, *"how"* questions and their bearing on the *"what"* question, which captures the essence of the firm's strategic purpose.

- The two frameworks are complementary and address the five building blocks of strategy introduced in the first chapter of this book.
- A final framework, the opportunity–response analysis framework, while not addressing the *"what"* question directly, does contribute insight relating to the *"when"* question, which reflects the temporal dimension of a firm's competitive position.

Notes

1. Drucker, P.F. (1994) The Theory of the Business, *Harvard Business Review*, September–October 1994 issue, pp. 95–104.
2. See Hamel, G. and Prahalad, C.K. (1989) Strategic Intent, *Harvard Business Review*, May–June; Prahalad, C.K. and Hamel, G. (1990) The Core Competence of the Corporation, *Harvard Business Review*, May–June 1989 issue.
3. Treacy, M. and Wiersema, F. (1995) *The Discipline of Market Leaders*, New York: Perseus Books.
4. Collis, D.J. and Rukstad, M.G. (2008) Can You Say What Your Strategy Is?, *Harvard Business Review*, April, pp. 82–90.
5. See *FORBES* (7 May 2012): Bezos is Best (*FORBES.com Views*).
6. DeGenaro, W. (1991) Business Intelligence Workshop for the Industrial Research Institute.
7. Andrews, K.R. (1971) *The Concept of Corporate Strategy*, New York: Richard D. Irwin.
8. Haberberg, A. (2000) Swatting SWOT (http://www2.wmin.ac.uk/haberba/SwatSWOT.htm; accessed 04.06.2012).
9. Teece, D.J. (2009) *Dynamic Capabilities & Strategic Management*, Oxford: Oxford University Press.
10. Teece, D.J., Pisano, G. and Shuen, A. (1997) Dynamic Capabilities and Strategic Management, *Strategic Management Journal*, 18(7), pp. 509–533.
11. Porter, M.E. (1980) Competitive Strategy: Techniques for Analyzing Industries and Competitors, New York: The Free Press.
12. Barney, J.B. and Clark, D.N. (2007) *Resource-Based Theory*, Oxford: Oxford University Press, pp. 69–71.
13. Grant, R.M. (1991) The Resource-Based Theory of Competitive Advantage: Implications for Strategy Formulation, *California Business Review*, Spring, pp. 114–135.

14. Peteraf, M.A. (1993) The Cornerstones of Competitive Advantage: A Resource-based View, *Strategic Management Journal*, Vol. 14, pp. 179–192.
15. Helfat, C.E, Finkelstein, S., Mitchell, W., Peteraf, M.A., Singh, H., Teece, D.J. and Winter, S.G. (2007) *Dynamic Capabilities*, Oxford: Blackwell Publishing.
16. Helfat, C.E and Peteraf, M.A. (2003) The Dynamic Resources-based View: Capability Life-cycles, *Strategic Management Journal*, Vol. 24, pp. 997–1010.
17. Helfat, C.E. and Peteraf, M.A. (2009) Understanding Dynamic Capabilities: Progress Along a Developmental Path, *Strategic Organization*, Vol. 7, pp. 91.
18. Whereas Grant (1991) draws a distinction between resources and capabilities, Birchall and Tovstiga (2005) view capabilities as a subset of the firm's (intellectual capital) resource base. Capabilities are viewed as a manifestation of (strategic and actionable) organizational knowledge and, as such, one possible expression of the firm's resources (Birchall, D.W. and Tovstiga, G. (2005) *Capabilities for Strategic Advantage – Leading through Technological Leadership*, Basingstoke: Palgrave Macmillan).

CHAPTER 6

Strategic Analysis III: Supporting-Level Sense Making

Reason does not work instinctively, but requires trial, practice, and instruction in order to gradually progress from one level of insight to another.

—Immanuel Kant

IN THIS CHAPTER, WE:

- elaborate on the nature, role and application of supporting-level frameworks of strategic analysis in the context of sense making;
- differentiate between supporting frameworks of analysis that probe and seek to provide insight on the firm's external competitive environment and those that focus on the firm-internal context;

- introduce some key supporting-level frameworks related to external and internal analysis;
- review and discuss the limitations of strategic analysis.

Strategic analysis is about sense making; it seeks to make sense of changes in the firm's external competitive environment that might require responsive action on the part of the firm. Good strategic analysis, we have argued earlier, begins with the framing of issues that are strategically relevant; these, in turn, give rise to strategic questions that demand to be addressed, if not resolved. It was further argued that it is always advisable to begin with a *high-level* positioning of the greater strategic context in question in order to "not lose sight of the wood for the trees". Two high-level conceptual approaches suitable for that task – the *value proposition* and *unique competing space* frameworks – were introduced and examined in Chapter 5. The outcome of the high-level analysis is a mapping of the firm's greater strategic context; it positions the external competitive environment and the firm's internal competitive position in the context of the strategic challenge at stake. The high-level analysis therefore establishes the greater strategic context for sense making. The firm's greater context consists of its external competitive environment on macro-economic, industry and market levels, and the internal context of the firm in question. Supporting-level frameworks of analysis provide this level of detail. Appropriately selected, they contribute elements of strategic insight prompted by the high-level analysis. Supporting-level frameworks of analysis focus on generating insights required for the sense making into either external or firm-internal factors, but generally not both.

Supporting-level Analysis: External and Internal Analysis Frameworks

The high-level frameworks of analysis – *the value proposition* and *unique competing space* frameworks – examined in Chapter 5 were shown to provide a big picture view of the firm's competitive context, which includes external and internal perspectives that converge on the core of the strategic challenge at stake. The *opportunity–response* framework also examined in Chapter 5 narrows the focus to the interplay between the firm's external environment and its internal basis of competitiveness. This latter approach introduces a dynamic and temporal perspective on the firm's competitive position.

Strategic analysis, we argued in Chapter 4, is about sense making. It is about generating insights prompted by framing the relevant issues and articulation of the "right" strategic questions. Individual analyses of the firm's external and internal basis of competitive context need to be purpose-led. The strategic analysis of these contexts is not an end unto itself; it is a means to an end. The objective is a reconstructed composite comprised of integrated insights reflecting the firm's competitive landscape. The application of individual frameworks of strategic analysis, whether externally or internally focused, therefore needs to be insight-driven. This demands astute selection and application of those frameworks that are most suitable to generating the insights sought. More importantly, though, it is the *integration* of insights generated through the application of individual frameworks of analysis that enables a better understanding of the firm's competitive context.

In this chapter we examine supporting frameworks of analysis that focus on the external context and those that can be used to make sense of the firm's internal context. There are many such frameworks of strategic analysis in circulation today. Entire Internet sites are devoted to management frameworks and models of analysis.[1] A number of these can be useful if appropriately applied, some are dated; all are limited by their simplification of reality and by the quality of the input data available when applying the analysis framework in question. Many frameworks related to strategy reflect the historical evolution of the strategy discipline. Early frameworks such as the *Ansoff product/market growth* and the *BCG growth share* matrices had their origins in the late 1950s and 1960s, respectively. While no doubt insightful at the time, more powerful frameworks have emerged. In the following sections a selection of supporting frameworks of analysis and their application will be examined.

The objective of the following sections of this chapter is not to provide the reader with an exhaustive compendium of supporting-level frameworks of analysis, of which many exist. Any of the recent good textbooks on strategic management can provide readers with an excellent overview.[2] The objective is much more to:

- Narrow the focus to a select few supporting frameworks of analysis that are representative of those that might be used to make sense of the firm's relevant external and internal competitive contexts;
- Explore how these might be applied to generate the insight prompted by strategic issues and questions articulated;
- Examine how insights from these relatively few frameworks can be integrated to create highly perceptive perspectives on a firm's competitive landscape.

The basic premises adhered to in the following sections are:

1. That a few frameworks, suitably selected and appropriately applied, can generate disproportionately valuable insight, and
2. That it is not necessarily the variety of the selection of frameworks; rather, what is important is the choice of frameworks and the way in which insights derived from these are integrated to generate a composite (albeit incomplete) of the firm's competitive situation in a way that most closely portrays the firm's competitive reality.

In the following two sections, therefore, only a few representative frameworks are introduced and discussed. More importantly, it is shown how insights from the relatively few frameworks selected can be *integrated* in a way that supports strategic sense making in a purposeful way.

Externally-focused Supporting Frameworks of Strategic Analysis

In this section we:

- Introduce a select few frameworks of strategic analysis focused on making sense of the firm's external competitive environment; in particular, these are frameworks that examine the firm's macro-economic, industry-, and market-level contexts relevant to its competitive position;
- Examine how these frameworks can be applied to support the high-level analysis frameworks introduced in the previous section;
- Discuss limitations of the frameworks within the greater context of strategic sense making.

At the outset of this book, in Chapter 1, we reflected on the purpose of an organization and what it seeks to achieve in order to meet the value expectations of its various stakeholder groups. Understanding what the organization is trying to achieve provides us with a frame of reference for assessing the external environmental factors that exert influence on the organization. This section first considers the external environment at the broader macro-economic level. We then examine the industry level of analysis. Industries are comprised of markets; hence, in the final part of this section we examine frameworks of analysis that are relevant to the firm's market level of analysis. A key tenet of the firm's external competitive context is that it is out of the direct control of any single firm. Nonetheless, industry-leading firms may very well wield some degree of influence in certain markets by virtue of their unique position in those markets. *Apple*'s influence on the smartphone market through the launch of its *iPhone* is a case in point. However, governmental regulatory bodies are always wary of firms that are in a position to exert power in their markets. For most firms the wider external environments within which they operate represent contexts over which they have no control. Forces in the wider external environment do not just drive sectors, industries and markets, however. They can have a powerful impact on evolving political and societal structures; these invariably carry important implications for the public sector and non-profit organizations.

The Macro-Economic Environment

To understand a particular sector and behaviors of market segments in that sector we need to develop an understanding of what is happening in the wider macro-economic environment. We need to understand what is happening, why it is happening, and how it will affect the firm's sector, industry and markets. The better we can understand the cause and effect associations between the forces shaping our business and its markets, the better placed we are to make strategic decisions to ensure effective future performance.

The PESTLE Framework

A *PESTLE* (acronym for *Political, Economic, Societal, Technological, Legal, Environmental*) analysis – sometimes appearing in its shorter *PEST* form – is always a suitable point of departure for making sense of the macro-economic environment of the firm. The factors that comprise this analysis are those that are thought to be strategically most relevant in assessing the macro-economic environment relevant to the firm. Strategy is about the future and it needs to focus on those things that might change the market for our goods and services. So, in assessing which of the *PESTLE* factors are relevant to a given analysis, it is important to focus on combinations of factors for which: (1) the probability of change is significant, and (2) the anticipated impact on the business is also significant. The second of the two criteria is the most important. Even if the probability of something happening is low, if it is anticipated to have a major impact on the firm's competitive position it should not be neglected in the strategic thinking and analysis. Developing a clear understanding of the cause and effect relationships between the factors in the *PESTLE* model is more challenging.

In reality, the *PESTLE* factors represent broad *categories* of factors. A typical analysis of the macro-economic context involves a large number of variables, many of which will be subject to constant change. It is therefore a complex activity that might involve both qualitative and quantitative analysis of data gathered. Firms often monitor change in the macro-economic environment with the help of a dashboard template that tracks key factors relevant to the firm's business activities. The key constraint, no matter how sophisticated the analysis, is always the validity and reliability of the data that is fed into the analysis. The dilemma facing many firms today – particularly those targeting emerging markets – is that there is simply no reliable data available. Hence, firms are more inclined toward adopting emergent approaches that narrow the analysis to the specific industry context over significantly shorter time horizons.

STRATEGY IN PRACTICE: WHEN CARRYING OUT AN ANALYSIS OF THE *PESTLE* FACTORS IT IS IMPORTANT TO KEEP THE FOLLOWING IN MIND:

- Not all *PESTLE* factors are equally relevant or important in respect to the specific analysis task at hand; it is important to narrow the primary focus on those that are. However, since competitive circumstances change, it is important not to neglect any of the factors.
- Of those factors relevant and important to the analysis, not all are changing at the same rate; some are evolving more quickly than others. It is important to track those that are changing most rapidly. Snapshot analyses offer a perspective frozen in time; trend analyses of the relevant factors offer more powerful views that suggest not only magnitude of change but also the direction of change.
- Most often macro-economic factors are interlinked; factors are interdependent and influence each other. It is

important to assess interactions between factors for a more integrated perspective on change in the macro-economic environment.

Sector and Industry-Level Analysis

Forces in the broader macro-economic environment of business invariably have an impact on the sector or industry environment in which an organization operates. While the macro-economic factors affect all industries, individual industries are affected in different ways. In this section we look at some dimensions relevant to the industry level of analysis. Two supporting frameworks of analysis are introduced: the *industry life-cycle (or maturity)* and the *industry value-chain analysis* frameworks. We examine how we might use these frameworks to gain a better understanding of the competitive dynamics of an industry and how these are affected by changes in that industry.

Industry Maturity, "S-Curve", or Life-cycle Analysis

The classic industry life-cycle model (sometimes referred to as the *industry "S" curve*) shows demand or performance (such as economic return on investment or market share) as a function of time. The life-cycle is typically segmented into four stages: *emergent*, *growth*, *maturity* and *decline* phases. In the emergent phase of the life-cycle, performance is often linked to a value offering that relates to some form of product functionality. Growth, initially, is likely to be slow. Customers are confined to the "*early adopters*" of new ideas and products. The *growth* period can be dramatic, with players seeking to meet the increase in demand while competing for a dominant position in the market. Eventually an industry moves into the *maturity* phase of the industry life-cycle, which is characterized by a flattening of the growth curve and a gradual commoditization of the value offering. Competition eventually focuses on pricing, and an increase in sales is possible only at the expense of the other players' market share. A maturing of the industry typically triggers a shakeout of competitors leading to a consolidation of the playing field. At this point the industry structure may resemble an oligopoly, dominated by a few large players. Finally, the industry moves into the decline phase as other newer products and solutions emerge.

The overall span of industry life-cycles and the duration of individual stages within them vary from industry to industry. The rate of industry evolution is tied to the characteristics unique to the industry sector. Industry sectors such as power generation may evolve over decades while the telecommunications sector might exhibit life-cycles of a half year. Generally, high-tech technology-related industries tend to have short life-cycles. While the *growth* phase of an industry life-cycle tends to be viewed as a favorable period, it may not be good for all players. Smaller players, unable to compete with the economies of scale or marketing budgets of the main players, can find themselves being squeezed out of a particular market. The *decline* phase, on the other hand, is not necessarily detrimental for everyone. First, this stage can go on for years; second, market leaders with favorable cost positions can often exploit and reap benefit from "*cash cow*" offerings in their product portfolio during this phase.

Different phases of the life-cycle offer varying opportunities for value creation and delivery. While the emergent and growth phases offer opportunity for competitive differentiation on value attributes other than price, competition in the maturity phase is typically characterized by eroding prices and margins. This latter stage is not an attractive situation to be in. Firms that compete successfully under these circumstances focus on operational excellence. Firms that don't achieve cost efficiency in this phase either exit or flounder.

STRATEGY IN PRACTICE: INDUSTRY LIFE-CYCLE ANALYSIS – LIMITATIONS

Life-cycle analysis enables us to make some projections on how an industry is likely to develop, and based on this, appropriate strategic approaches in each phase. But, there are limitations:

- The relative length of each of the life-cycle phases varies significantly from industry to industry. Some, such as the building and hotel industries, have been in maturity for decades without showing signs of decline.
- Not all industries go through exactly the same process; maturing trends can be reversed either by new social and/or technological trends. Industries can reinvent themselves producing resurgence in demand, as evidenced by *Nespresso* coffee, *Häagen-Daz* luxury ice cream, or *easyJet* with low cost flights.
- Some industries (such as fashion and media) can exert a powerful impact on demand and are relatively immune to economic cycling. Others may exhibit a cyclical pattern of rapid growth followed by equally rapid decline in response to change in the socio-economic environment.

Industry Value Chain Analysis

Industries are comprised of a series of value-adding sectors. These are sometimes thought of as *primary* (e.g. raw materials extraction), *secondary* (e.g. processing and manufacturing), *tertiary* (e.g. provision of services) and *quaternary* (e.g. provision of scientific and engineering research). An industry value chain analysis provides insight on where value is created in a particular sector or across an entire industry. It represents an ordering of the players that comprise the industry. Players along the value chain contribute different elements to the creation of the value offering generated in an industry. Value is created along the entire length of the value chain. However, the distribution of where value is created along the value chain varies along its length. Value creation is typically concentrated at specific points along the industry value chain; the location of these points depends on the evolutionary stage of the industry in question. This gives rise to value creation "hot spots" along the value chain. These are points along the value chain in which value creation is disproportionately concentrated. Furthermore, these value "hot spots" tend to migrate as the industry matures. Typically, value creation is concentrated in upstream segments of the value chain in the early stages of an industry. As an industry matures its value "hot spots" tend to migrate downstream along the value chain.

An analysis of the firm's industry value chain delivers important insights that can be used in a number of ways. The analysis can be used to identify where the value "hot spots" exist along the firm's industry value chain. Once located, the firm can appraise where it is positioned relative to the "hot spots". Once this has been established, the firm can use these insights to derive suitable options that might include, for example, a suitable repositioning of the firm along the value chain. Migration of the value creation "hot spot" that accompanies the maturing of an industry often triggers movement within the value chain; this might involve integration within the value chain segment (horizontal integration) or along the value chain (vertical integration).

STRATEGY IN PRACTICE: INDUSTRY VALUE CHAIN "HOT SPOTS"

Value creation, we have argued earlier in this section, is not equally distributed along the industry value chain. This gives rise to value creation "hot spots", prompting the following important questions as firm's reflect on their industry value chain and, more importantly, their position in the industry value chain:

- Where, in your industry's value chain, is the value creation "hot spot" at this point in time?
- What is the link between value creation "hot spot" and the industry's key success factors; that is, what are the key success factors that define the segment of the value chain hosting the value "hot spot"?
- Where in the value chain is the firm positioned relative to the industry's value "hot spot"; what are the implications

of the maturity stage of the industry for competition in that industry?

- To what extent is the value "hot spot" migrating?
- Does the migration of the value "hot spot" represent an opportunity or a threat for the firm?
- What are the implications of the firm's position in the industry value chain for its unique competing space; that is, the firm's ability to carve out a unique window of opportunity for value creation and delivery?

Market-Level Analysis

Industries typically encompass a number of markets. The automotive industry, for example, is comprised of markets ranging from low cost, compact vehicles to exclusive luxury limousines. The focus of the analysis of the following three frameworks is at the market level. This is where the firm faces its competition directly.

Key Success Factor Analysis

Key success factors (KSFs) are those competing factors that most closely capture the competitive essence of a market place. A good understanding of these offers a potentially powerful perspective on the market in question. Key success factors encompass the *"rules of the market place"* and are those factors that carry the greatest implications for success and performance of the firm in its respective market. Key success factors might also be viewed as those factors that capture the *"market place logic"* – the underlying rationale for what constitutes successful competition in a particular market. Factors might include unique product attributes, or unique capabilities combined with other strategic assets such as a strong brand. In mature markets, the ability of players in that market to operate at a low cost basis may be a key success factor. Often, a combination of factors form clusters of key success factors. Key success factors are attributes of the market place. No individual player "owns" the key success factors of a given market; however, individual players may profoundly influence their evolution. A case in point is the influence *Apple's iPhone* exerted in the smartphone market. Once introduced, the *iPhone* set the standard for all competitors in the smartphone market.

Key success factors represent the market needs and expectations on which the firm must deliver if it is to be successful; firms succeed by virtue of their ability to deliver on the key success factors that characterize their respective markets. Firms that have been successful over long periods of time in stable markets often fall prey to losing their position when market conditions change unexpectedly. Even the most successful of companies, however, find it difficult to sustain competitive advantage indefinitely. This is because as markets evolve and change, the underlying key success factors change as well. Key success factors can be thought of as having a finite "shelf life". Firm's often fail to recognize this and fall into the *legacy thinking* trap. They fail to update their understanding of the market's evolving competitive characteristics as they continue competing on obsolete key success factors.

Key success factors are sometimes confused with *key performance indicators* (KPIs). The latter lie clearly within the domain of an individual firm, whereas *key success factors* are attributes of the market place. *Key performance indicators* might be thought of as a measure of the firm's ability to respond to the *key success factors* of the firm's market place.

Key success factors capture the essence of customers' needs; these might be obvious, but in some cases, customers may not yet "know" their needs. Firms and organizations that are in a position to pre-emptively fulfill these needs stand to achieve competitive advantage. Another perspective on this: key success factors of a market encompass the *criteria* that define the firm's *unique competing space* for a particular market. Firms that succeed in delivering on these criteria better than their competitors thereby establish their unique competing space. By extension, key success factors intrinsically corroborate the uniqueness and superiority of a firm's differentiated value proposition, if valid.

Key success factors can be categorized into *qualifiers* and *order winners*. *Qualifiers* might be thought of as *"license to play"* factors that a player in the market must deliver on in order to compete in that market at all, though they do not ensure success for that player. On the other hand, *order winning* key success factors are of the *"license to win"* type. The ability to deliver on *order winning* key success factors provides the firm with a competitive edge in its markets. A firm needs to fulfill both qualifying and order winning key success factors; however, it achieves success on the basis of the latter. As markets evolve and the competition encroaches on a firm's unique competitive position, the firm's *order winning* key success factors gradually degrade to *qualifying* factors.

Key success factors are critical elements of the market level of analysis. They reflect and resonate with those unique market demand attributes that determine the firm's *unique competing space*. In the context of the *value proposition* framework, key success factors contribute vital insight to the *"where?"* and *"what?"* questions. Finally, key success factors provide critical constituents of the market opportunity trajectory in the *opportunity–response* framework.

STRATEGY IN PRACTICE: A KEY SUCCESS FACTORS ASSESSMENT

The following questions probe the key success factor in your firm's markets:

- What are the *order winning* key success factors in your firm's markets, and how do these define the value offering at the core of the market's expectation? How are these changing?

- What are the *qualifying* key success factors?
- What are the key assumptions made in your industry about its *order winning* and *qualifying* key success factors?
- How quickly are the key success factors in your firm's markets changing?
- How is your firm identifying and monitoring the key success factors of its markets; how is it detecting emerging key success factors?

Competitor Analysis and Competitive Intelligence

Alongside efforts to gain a better understanding of their customer base and its needs, firms need to continually monitor and make sense of their competitors' activities and positions. In highly competitive markets the gathering and analysis of competitor intelligence is an important strategic activity. One way of prioritizing competitor intelligence analysis is to focus on time horizons. Shorter business cycles usually require focus on current and existing competitors, whereas longer business cycles call for the analysis of potential new entrants and substitute products or services.

Competitor analysis can be applied to predict how competitors might behave and how they might react to a firm's own future strategy. Competitors can be assessed on the basis of the following dimensions (Grant, 2010[3]):

- *Strategy:* On what basis are competitors competing; what *key success factors* are they focusing on; what is it that sets them apart?
- *Objectives:* In what direction do competitors' appear to be moving – and with what objectives? To what extent is their performance meeting these objectives? How are competitors' objectives likely to evolve?
- *Assumptions:* What assumptions do competitors hold about the industry and themselves? What "industry logic" are competitors' adhering to?
- *Resources and capabilities:* What are the competitors' key strengths and weakness; what are their vulnerabilities?

Competitors' reactions to the firm's strategy are prompted by the following questions:

- What strategic changes will competitors initiate?
- How will competitors respond to our strategic initiatives?

The *key success factor* analysis introduced in the previous section provides a potentially insightful platform for conducting a comparative competitor analysis.[4] In a first step, key success factors are identified, prioritized and ranked in terms of *importance* (columns "*1a*" and "*1b*" in Figure 6.1). In a second step, the relative performance (columns "*2a*", "*3a*" and "*4a*") of the firm and its competitors "A" and "B" on each of the key success factors is appraised. Scores are then formed for each of the competitors by multiplying the *importance* (common to all competitors for each key success factor) by the individual competitors' *performance* for each of the key success factor (columns "*a* × *b*"; for example, for the firm: "*2a*" × "*2b*"). Summed scores are then formed by adding up individual scores of the firm and its competitors (columns "*2b*", "*3b*" and "*4b*", respectively). The summed scores of each of the competitors are then compared. The higher the final summed score, the better the competitive performance of the competitor in question.

The comparative competitor analysis based on key success factors can be a useful tool. First, it encourages managers to reflect critically on the precise definition of the market in question. Only once this is clear does it make sense to identify the market's attributes such as its key success factors. Second, regardless of the numerical outcome generated, the analysis focuses managers' attention and debate on the essential strategic elements pertaining to market in questions – its attributes, evolution, competitors and the firm's own competitive position relative to all of these. Even if all this leads to is an agreement on what the disagreement is about, the analysis will at least have succeeded in ensuring that managers are on the same page – which often is a significant achievement in its own right.

COMPARATIVE COMPETITOR PERFORMANCE

KSFs (ranked)	IMPORTANCE[1] (a)	OWN FIRM		COMPETITOR 'A'		COMPETITOR 'B'	
		Performance[2] (b)	Score (a x b)	Performance (b)	Score (a x b)	Performance (b)	Score (a x b)
1.	1a	1b	2a	2b	3a	3b	4a	4b
2.								
3.								
etc.								

Comparative Scores: | Own Firm Σ [a x b] | Firm 'A' Σ [a x b] | Firm 'B' Σ [a x b]

Notes:

[1] Importance ranking (weighting) on a scale of 1 to 5 (5 = most important; 1 = least important)

[2] Performance estimation (how well the firm in question performs on this KSF) on a scale of 1 to 5 (5 = excellent performance; 1 = poor performance)

Figure 6.1 Comparative competitor analysis on the basis of a key success factor analysis. (1) Importance ranking (weighting) on a scale of 1 to 5 (5 = most important; 1 = least important); (2) performance estimation (how well the firm in question performs on the respective KSF) on a scale of 1 to 5 (5 = excellent; 1 = poor)

The comparative competitor analysis presents challenges. More often than not, the relevant key success factors are not numerically quantifiable. The appraisal of subjective measures relies on solicitation of perceptions. Reliable insights demand that the "right" questions are asked. Finally, it goes without saying that, ultimately, validation of the key success factors must be solicited from and provided by the market place.

STRATEGY IN PRACTICE: COMPETITOR INTELLIGENCE: CLUSTER ANALYSIS

Strategic cluster analysis is an alternative approach to monitoring competitive activity in a firm's sphere of business activities; it compares and provides a visual picture of the strategies of clusters of companies in a similar industry. It is useful in a number of respects:

- In highly competitive industries with many competitors it may be difficult to track the activity of individual players. A clustering of competitors can help firms not to lose sight of trends that activities of individual competitors might not suggest.
- Clustering competitors into groups with comparable strategies can help build an understanding of how a particular industry operates, and why some companies appear to share common strategies, and why certain strategies appear unsustainable.
- A clustering approach enables a projection into the future by providing clues about the emerging competitive landscape and what it might look like.

The Porter "Five Forces"' Framework

The origin of Porter's "five forces"[5,6] framework dates back to the late 1970s. The framework reflects the *structure–conduct–performance* paradigm of industrial organization economics prevalent in that era. This paradigm views the structure of an industry or market as a key determinant of the state of competition in that context. Firms' conduct – that is, their strategy – is determined by the nature of competition in their respective competitive contexts. The "five forces" represent structural forces that determine the attractiveness (e.g. profitability potential) of a market place. The associated analysis places the emphasis on identifying the "right industry" and within that the attractive positions. It provides an external perspective that is most suitable for a market-level analysis. It is less suitable for an industry group or sector-level analysis, unless that industry features similar or comparable value offerings. Although dated, the "five forces" analysis can provide valuable insights in the nature of competition in a market and, by extension, the attractiveness of that market from the firm's perspective.

Essentially, the "five forces" analysis framework is comprised of an industry value chain that features two possible entry points; one representing the threat of new entrants, and the other the threat of substitution of the value offering in question.

The framework has limitations, however. Our understanding of the determinants of industry rivalry, market dynamics and competitive behavior of firms has progressed substantially since the framework was proposed. Value chains are becoming ever more complex; organizations are engaging simultaneously in competition and selective collaboration (a constellation sometimes referred to as "co-opetition"). There is also an increase in the number of multiple and complementary relationships firms engage in. An example is the array of relationships between Microsoft and Intel for mutual gain. Indeed, many industries can be viewed as complex networks of mutually dependent players in which niche players play an important role in complementing the market leaders. An example is Adobe, the software firm, which has succeeded in developing a niche market because its products were differentiated and did not challenge industry standards, such as Microsoft Word.

In other words, our conception of competition and its multiple complex expressions has changed considerably from the time when the "five forces" framework was first proposed. Consequently, Porter's framework has been criticized mainly for its assumptions; including unrealistic conjectures that:

- Players in the value chain – suppliers, competitors and buyers – are unrelated and that they do not interact;
- The source of advantage underpinning the value offering at stake is related to the industry or market structure; and
- The level of complexity and ambiguity in the market is low, so that players can readily stage and respond to competitors' moves.

Also limiting is the "five forces" framework's neglect of the individual firms' resource base; the internal competitive basis of the individual firm and the implications of these factors for the nature of competition. Finally, the Porter "five forces" framework has been shown to be of limited application in the context of third and public sector organizations that do not "compete" in the conventional sense.

Internally-Focused Supporting Frameworks of Strategic Analysis

The firm's external environment is undoubtedly an important determinant of the firm's strategic position. Arguably, however, the firm's internal factors are even more important. Empirical studies suggest that external industry effects explain about 20% of a firm's superior performance while factors reflecting the firm's basis of competitiveness within its competitive context account for between 30 and 35% of its performance.[7] In this section we explore the firm's internal basis of competitiveness and its implications for the firm's ability to establish and nurture a position of competitive advantage, its *unique competing space*. To that end, the frameworks examined in this section support sense making by generating insight into those factors that determine the firm's (ideally, uniquely differentiated) internal context. The firm's internal context is comprised of its assets (traditional resources, capabilities, knowledge) as well as its formal and informal structure, infrastructure, processes and culture and, ultimately, its leadership and management capability. The purpose of the frameworks examined in this section is to provide insight into these factors.

The *resource-based theory* of the firm encompasses the key perspective on the firm's internal analysis. Hence the essential internally-focused supporting frameworks of analysis address various aspects of the firm's resource base and the associated organizational elements. The frameworks probe the disposition, ability and capacity to exploit its unique bundles of strategic resources.

With reference to the high-level sense making frameworks presented in Chapter 5, the *value proposition* and the *unique competing space* frameworks, the internal analysis represents the final missing element of analysis required for completion of the firm's competitiveness-related "bigger picture".

Strategic Resources and the Resource-Based View (RBV)

Firms differentiate themselves on the basis of their unique resource position and the way in which they uniquely configure and exploit their resources. The resulting superior value thus generated by the firm, in turn, endows substance and validity to the firm's *value proposition*. It provides scope and breadth of the firm's unique competing space. Both the firm's *value proposition* and its *unique competing space* are thereby critically coupled to the firm's strategic resource position, and its ability to configure and exploit this resource base in uniquely differentiated ways. The notion of *asymmetries* – that is, differences in the firm's ability to configure and exploit its resource position – plays an important role in this regard.

The resource-based view (RBV), sometimes also referred to as the resource-based theory of the firm, is critically related to the firm's value proposition and unique competing space. The resource-based view states that " . . . all organizations can build and maintain long-term strategic advantage as a result of exploiting bundles of valued resources that other organizations cannot readily imitate".[8-12]

The firm's *strategic* resources are those that enable it to differentiate itself competitively; they enable the firm to deliver on the *order-winning* key success factor. Firms invariably have capabilities of the *enabling* or *supporting* type. While these enable the firm to address the *qualifying* key success factors of its market place, they are not sufficient for achieving any significant degree of competitive advantage. The resource-based view argues that where a firm is in a leading competitive position, or is building market share, there must be a reason why it is in a position to do this. That reason is to be found in the way in which the firm configures and deploys its unique (in the sense of rare, valuable and difficult-to-imitate) resources.

The approaches to the analysis and appraisal of the firm's internal resource based proposed by Grant[3] and Grant and Jordan[13] are particularly useful. A number of the frameworks introduced and discussed in the following sections are derived from these authors' work.

Capabilities as Strategic Resources

From a resource-based perspective, the firm's capabilities are assets of the intangible type. Embedded in the firm's intellectual capital, capabilities might be thought of as manifestations of organizational knowledge. They are of strategic relevance to the firm if they draw on strategically relevant knowledge. Capabilities are complex; they are derived from distinctive skills, skill sets and experiential knowledge. If strategically relevant, capabilities enable the firm to establish, exploit and expand its unique competing space.

Capabilities have been defined to consist of bundles of constituent skills and technologies – rather than single discrete skills or technologies – that create disproportionate value for the customer, differentiate its owner from competitors and allow entrance to new markets.[14] Moreover, capabilities represent an accumulation of learning over time; that is to say that they are path-dependent. *Path-dependency* relates to the way in which capabilities evolve and develop. Capabilities do not emerge over night; it takes deliberate effort to shape and nurture them. Clearly, the organizational context in which they evolve – the existing resource and capabilities base, the culture of the organization, its leadership – all contribute to the shaping of and ability of the firm to exploit its capabilities.

A well-managed portfolio of knowledge-based capabilities is a prerequisite for building a strong and sustainable competitive advantage. Key competitive knowledge – primarily tacit knowledge embedded in complex organizational routines and evolving from experience over time – tends to be unique and difficult to replicate, imitate and transfer. These features of a capability carry a number of important implications for competitive differentiation. One of these has to do with the ease with which a capability can be replicated, transferred or lost to a competitor. For example, a high degree of *tacitness* can be an effective barrier to diffusion of knowledge. From the external perspective, this represents a protective mechanism; however, for internal operations, knowledge transfer and sharing often represent challenges to be overcome. Firms must nurture mechanisms for consciously and deliberately managing their stock of tacit knowledge.

Of Leonard-Barton's[15] proposed four interdependent dimensions describing the composition of capabilities two relate to knowledge competence repositories: these consist of (1) people-embodied knowledge and skills, and (2) physical technical systems. The remaining two represent organizational knowledge-control and -channeling mechanisms: these are comprised of (3) managerial systems, and (4) organizational culture, values and norms.

Managing capabilities strategically extends beyond management of any individual capability. The firm's stock of capabilities typically consists of clusters, within which individual capabilities may be interlinked. Hence, it is useful to think of the firm's capabilities in terms of its portfolio of capabilities. Constituent capabilities may be of varying maturity and strategic impact. Various views on the portfolio perspective on capabilities have been proposed in the past. A capabilities portfolio mapping approach proposed by Birchall and Tovstiga[16] recommends a strategic positioning of the firm's portfolio of capabilities in terms of competitive impact (emerging, pacing, key or obsolete) and competitive position (that is, the firm's degree of control over its portfolio of capabilities and its ability to exploit its current portfolio).

STRATEGY IN PRACTICE: YOUR FIRM'S STRATEGIC CAPABILITIES

You may wish to reflect on the capabilities in your own organization:

- What is your business unit or team particularly good at doing?
- What is it that your customers value particularly about what you do?
- What skills and other assets underpin this success?
- How rare are the associated strategic capabilities?
- How easily would your competitors be able to imitate these, and how can you make it more difficult for competitors to imitate what your firm does uniquely well?
- What issues and challenges emerge as you seek to transfer, embed and reinforce strategically critical skills and knowledge throughout the firm?

Dynamic Capabilities

Competitive environments change and so too must the firm's portfolio of strategic capabilities. They must be flexible and responsive to changing customer demands, as well as new and emerging market opportunities. Dynamic capabilities have been defined as the ability that underpins the capacity of organizations to shape, reshape, configure and reconfigure their strategic resources and capabilities in response to changes in their competitive environment.[17,18] Teece's[18] conceptualization of three key activities associated with dynamic capabilities was introduced in the previous chapter in the context of the *opportunity–response* analysis framework. Dynamic capabilities are arguably a class of capabilities in their own right; they are instrumental in the renewal and upgrading of the firm's primary capabilities.

Identifying the Firm's Strategic Resources

The firm's strategic resources can be divided into two main categories. In the first we find the traditional *tangible* resources such as physical and financial resources; they are the "land, labor, capital" traditional, primary factors of production. These resources for the most part can be characterized as *"having"* resources; resources that can be readily accounted for on a balance sheet. In the second category we find the firm's *intangible* assets; these are sometimes characterized as the firm's *"doing"* assets. Strictly speaking, these are not assets in the traditional accounting sense. In practice, these assets express themselves as the firms' ability to "do" things (ideally differently); they are knowledge or manifestations of knowledge such as capability or competence, or other intellectual capital-bound assets such as brand. Capabilities and competencies are embedded in the firm's intellectual capital; this, in turn, is comprised of its *human*, *structural* and *relational* capital.

Key to the notion of the firm's strategic resources, whether based on "having" or "doing" type, is the strategic *relevance* of these to the firm's capacity and ability to establish a position of competitive advantage. Physical and financial assets have been the means by which firms have traditionally established their competitive position. In many physical asset-intensive industries, this is still the case. Industries such as mining, oil exploration and production, and automotive manufacturing are highly dependent on physical and financial assets. Even in the services sector, where the value offering is typically intangible, the relationship-based physical factors such as location and facilities can be important factors on the basis of which firms competing in these markets seek to differentiate themselves.

Increasingly, however, the "doing" category of resources is being recognized for its ever greater and critical contribution to the firm's sustainable competitiveness. There are numerous indicators suggesting as much. If one examines the relationship between the *book-to-market* value ratio (sometimes referred to as "Tobin's q") of firms traded on any of the world's stock exchanges, one sees that the proportion of the intangible part of a typical firm's market capitalization has grown disproportionately since the early 1980s. In some cases, the intangible portion of a firm's market valuation can be as high as 80% or more.[19] This introduces a high degree of volatility to the firm's traded market value. In recent times this has led to several stock market crashes – or "rupturing of the bubble" – as in the early 2000s and in the more recent economic crisis. Despite the vulnerabilities of high intellectual asset valuations, knowledge and its manifestations as capabilities and competencies are increasingly viewed to be at the root of wealth creation.

The firm's strategic resources and capabilities, as argued earlier, are those with significant impact on the firm's ability to create and sustain a position of competitive advantage. As suggested in Figure 6.2, the firm's strategic resources and capabilities also resonate with its markets' *order-winning* key success factors.

Figure 6.2 shows a broad breakdown of the firm's resources and capabilities; those that are strategic are shown to contribute to the firm's position of competitive advantage.

Building on the broad categorization indicated in Figure 6.2 we can proceed to identify the firm's stock of resources and capabilities on

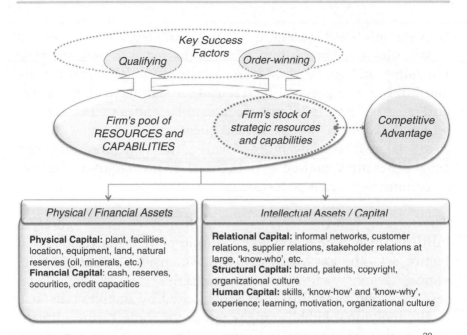

Figure 6.2 Firm's resources and capabilities; tangible and intanglibe assets[20]

the basis of a semi-quantitative analysis as suggested in Figure 6.3 . The firm's resources with significant presence in the firm are broadly categorized according to their type – tangible and intangible, and subsequently in terms of their more specific designation. In a first step, all resources with significance presence in the

Illustrative Example		Resource with significant presence in firm (a)	Strategic Relevance[1] (b)	Firm's relative strength in this resource[2] (c)
	Resource Category			
Tangibles	Physical capital	P1	7	8
		P2	6	6
	Financial capital	F1	5	7
Intangibles	Human capital	H1	3	4
		H2	6	4
	Relational capital	R1	8	9
		R2	7	7
	Structural capital	S1	8	4
		S2	7	6

Notes:
1) Strategic relevance: 1 = irrelevant; 10 = highly relevant
2) Relative strength: 1 = very weak; 10 = very strong

Figure 6.3 Semi-quantitative approach to identifying and appraising the firm's strategic resources and capabilities[21]

firm are thus listed in column *"a"*. In a next step, all resources and capabilities listed in column *"a"* are appraised as to their *strategic relevance*; the estimated values on a scale of 1 to 10 (1 representing absolutely no impact; 10 representing a significant impact) are entered in column *"b"*. *Strategic relevance* relates to the degree to which the resource of capability in question has an impact on the firm's competitive advantage. Finally, the same resources and capabilities are appraised as to their relative strength in the firm in column *"c"*; again on a scale of 1 to 10.

The summary of the appraisal of the firm's resources and capabilities can then be plotted on a simple matrix chart such as in Figure 6.4. The axes represent the dimensions "strategic relevance" (*x-axis*) and "relative strength" (*y-axis*). Individual resources and capabilities are represented by bubbles; the size of the individual bubbles might represent some further dimension, such as the investment effort in that resource or capability.

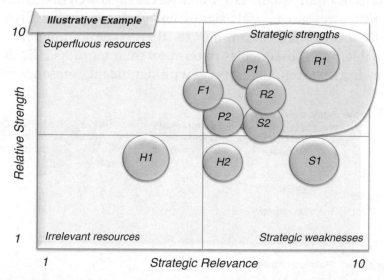

Figure 6.4 Graphical appraisal of firm's strategic resources; identification of strategic relevance and strength of firm in respect of resources and capabilities. (Note: the figure is based on the illustrative performance ratings of resources and capabilities in Figure 6.3[22])

Ideally, the appraisal should indicate a clustering of the firm's resources in the upper right quadrant. This is where the resources identified are not only appraised to be strategically relevant, but the firm is also in a strong position relative to its competitors in respect of these resources and capabilities.

In the illustrative case shown graphically in Figure 6.4 , most of the resources and capabilities are positioned in the upper right-hand quadrant, which is where they are not only of strategic relevance, but the firm is also in a strong position in respect of each of the resources in question. However, resources "*H1*", "*H2*" and "*S1*" are shown to be in the lower left and lower right quadrants, respectively. The firm would be advised to invest effort in moving resources "*H2*" and "*S1*" into the upper right quadrant as these are strategically relevant. "*H1*", on the other hand, is largely irrelevant, hence the firm would be advised either to phase out this resource, or to invest significantly with the intent of moving it diagonally upwards towards the upper right quadrant.

As with all mappings of this kind, one can gain further insight by tracking the evolution of individual resources and capabilities over time; one can also indicate inter-relationships (dependencies) between individual resources. Finally, one can also plot comparable resources of key competitors for comparative purposes.

Appraising the Firm's Strategic Resources and Capabilities

The frameworks introduced and discussed in the previous section enable an identification and first appraisal of the firm's strategic resources. Despite the fact that many resources are difficult to appraise due to their intangible character, resources and capabilities can be subjected to a more precise appraisal. Two approaches to a more precise appraisal of the firm's resources and capabilities are introduced and discussed in this section: Grant's "profit-earning potential" of a resource of capability, and the "*VRIO*" (valuable, rare, imitable, organization) framework.

Grant's Profit-Earning Potential of a Resource or Capability

Grant's[3,13] approach to appraising the strategic importance of an individual resource or capability relates the strategic relevance and importance of a resource or capability to its "profit-earning potential". Three conditions fulfill this criterion: (1) the extent to which the resource or capability contributes to establishment of competitive advantage in the firm; (2) the degree to which it does so sustainably; and (3) the appropriability of that resource and capability. The three conditions are further subdivided into eight criteria as shown in Figure 6.5.

How does one apply this framework? Individual resources – for example, those identified with the help of the frameworks discussed in the previous section – are individually appraised on the eight factors ("scarcity" through to "embeddedness"). A scoring column for noting estimated performance of the individual resource or capability on each of the criteria is indicated in Figure 6.5.

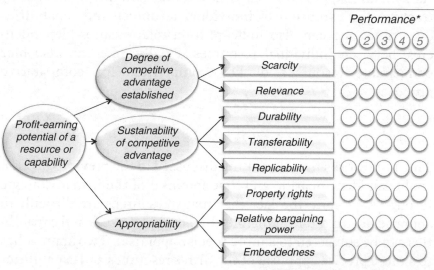

Performance: '1' = poor; '5' = excellent

Figure 6.5   Grant's "*profit-earning potential*" framework for appraising strategic importance of a resource/capability[3,13]

Clearly, most if not all of the eight criteria indicated are subjective in nature; hence, a semi-quantitative estimation of performance is often the best we can achieve. However, even an estimated performance score on any of the criteria for a particular resource or capability, if carefully reflected and appropriately debated, can provide valuable insight.

This framework requires each resource or capability to be appraised individually. Estimations of "strategic relevance" of resources or capabilities identified and subjected to a first appraisal on the basis of the semi-structured approach described in the previous section can thereby be assessed with greater confidence.

The VRIO Framework

The VRIO (*Valuable, Rare, Imitable, Organization*) framework proposed by Barney and Hesterley[11] presents an alternative means of appraising the competitive impact of a resource or capability. The framework is shown in Figure 6.6. It can be used in a manner similar to the previously discussed framework. Individual resources and capabilities are systematically scrutinized for their competitive impact.

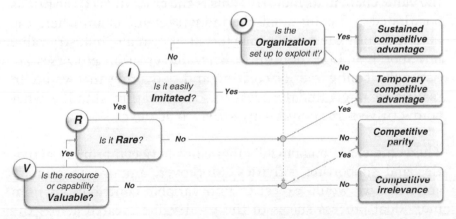

Figure 6.6   *VRIO* framework for systematic appraisal of strategic relevance of individual resources and capabilities[11]

Individual resources or capabilities are probed for how valuable, rare and imitable they are; a final step of the algorithm queries the extent to which the organization is enabled to exploit the resource or capability. This final step resonates with the fifth building of strategy introduced in Chapter 1 of this book. The implication is important: a firm may be in possession of resources or capabilities that are valuable, rare and not easily imitated; yet if it is incapable of exploiting the resource or capability, possession of the same may endow temporary advantage at best.

Analysis of the Firm's (Internal) Value Chain

In a previous section we introduced the *industry-level value chain* and saw how its analysis provides insight on where value creation is concentrated along the chain. Similarly, firms have internal value chains. The internal value chain provides insight into how the firm is utilizing its processes, resources and capabilities to create the value it delivers to the market. A generic framework of the firm's internal value chain attributed to Porter[6] provides a visual mapping of the alignment of the firm's value creating activities and processes.

Ideally, the firm's internal value chain aligns strategically with the value chain in its industry. This is the case when (1) the firm is positioned at a point along the industry value chain where the potential to create value is high (i.e. at or near an "industry value hot spot"), and (2) the firm's own value-creation processes are optimally configured for creating and delivering that value. In reality, we rarely find this idealized constellation – but it is what competitive firms continually strive to achieve.

The value chain mapping distinguishes between primary activities and supporting activities. Moreover, among the primary activities we would expect to find variable contributions from individual process stages to the total value created across the firm's value chain. It should be the strategic objective of the firm to align and focus its effort on those of its activities that contribute most significantly to where the potential for creating value is greatest in the industry value chain. In some cases this might lead to a migration of the firm's activities downstream along its industry value chain – or possible relocating the firm in an entirely new industry.

STRATEGY IN PRACTICE: YOUR FIRM'S INTERNAL VALUE CHAIN

Here is an exercise you may wish to do to help you understand your organization's value chain and its competitive implications:

- Map your organization's internal value chain and external value net, or value system.
- Identify value creation "hot spots" in your firm's internal and external value chains and the parts of the chain, or linkages, where significant value is being created and delivered.
- Identify the nature of value creation at these "value hot spots". What are the possible strategic implications of their location for your firm?
- What are your organization's value creating capabilities in relation to where the "value hot spots" are situated – both externally and internally?
- How are the "value hot spots" evolving and shifting? How vulnerable do these changes leave your firm – and why so?

The Formal and Informal Organization: "Getting the Organizational Act Together"

In this final section we examine the organizational context within which the firm seeks to exploit its resources and capabilities for the purpose of securing and potentially expanding its unique competing space. The organizational context is arguably the least accessible domain of analysis; much of what really

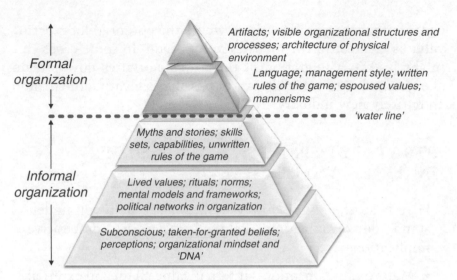

Formal organization

Informal organization

Artifacts; visible organizational structures and processes; architecture of physical environment

Language; management style; written rules of the game; espoused values; mannerisms

'water line'

Myths and stories; skills sets, capabilities, unwritten rules of the game

Lived values; rituals; norms; mental models and frameworks; political networks in organization

Subconscious; taken-for-granted beliefs; perceptions; organizational mindset and 'DNA'

Figure 6.7 "Iceberg" model of the organization: formal and informal organization

matters strategically remains hidden to the eye. Many of the relevant factors contributing to a firm's internal basis of competitiveness are situated below the organization's "waterline" as suggested in Figure 6.7, which is sometimes referred to as the "iceberg" model of the organization.[23] These factors include attributes of the organization that extend beyond the firm's resources and capabilities to include its structure, processes, practices, routines, culture and, ultimately, leadership and management styles.

Critically, these elements need to be in alignment in order for the firm to achieve any degree of competitiveness. Needless to point out, the most strategically relevant resources and capabilities are of little use to an organization that fails to "get its act together". A military analogy is useful here: sophisticated weaponry in the hands of those incapable of using it is essentially useless. So it is with organizations seeking to establish their competitive position – the firm's resources and capabilities can unfold their full competitive potential only if and when the organizational context is optimally aligned with this purpose.

The iceberg model suggests different levels of the organization, only the tip of which is apparent to the visible eye. The essence of the organization – embodying its culture – lies largely in its informal part. This is where we find the organization's stock of strategically relevant knowledge, its intellectual assets embodying human, structural and relational capital – and its culture. The informal organizational levels are essentially impossible to "manage" in the traditional sense of the word; the best we can do is to create and nurture enabling conditions that allow the organization to unfold its full competitive potential. In practice, that is much easier said than done.

STRATEGY IN PRACTICE: ON USING FRAMEWORKS OF STRATEGIC ANALYSIS

- *Pieces of the bigger picture.* First, all frameworks, models and techniques are simplifications of reality; hence we need to challenge their applicability for a given analysis as much as we need to challenge the quality of the inputs once we decide to use them. Appropriately used, each framework delivers a piece of insight, however small. These are the pieces of the greater picture we are trying to assemble. However, the insights are only as valid and as reliable as the information that goes into the analysis. It is the cumulative picture assembled from the various bits of insights that we are ultimately seeking. Selecting the appropriate framework, carrying out a good analysis and then assembling the pieces require practice and skill.

- *Trends, not snapshots.* Second, many frameworks such as the *PESTLE* analysis, *key success factor* analysis and *value chain* analyses (both industry and internal) are most often used simply to develop a snapshot analysis at any point in time. Substantially more powerful insights can be gained by extending these analyses to trend analyses. Trend analyses tell stories in a way that snapshots cannot. When mapping out a simple *PESTLE* analysis graphically, indicating trends by simple vectors (e.g. direction of arrow indicating general direction of change; length of arrow indicating magnitude of change) adds significantly to the transparency and expressiveness of the analysis.

- *Singing from the same hymn sheet.* Finally, the real value in carrying out an analysis does not necessarily lie in the absolute correctness of the analysis outcome. In many situations, such as in the case of emerging markets, no amount of analysis will produce an absolutely "right" answer. The real value of the analysis then lies in the focus and discipline it brings to the thinking and debate around the boardroom table, even if the outcome is "agreement on what the disagreement is about". To that end, appropriate analysis frameworks – particularly when brought to flipchart or whiteboard – can help to channel thinking, help senior managers to align their thinking and to effectively "sing off the same hymn sheet".

Limitations

As with all frameworks, the purpose and usefulness of the *opportunity–response* framework lies first and foremost in the guidance it can provide to our strategic thinking. It necessarily provides a simplified and therefore distorted picture of reality. This we need to keep in mind at all times. Market opportunities invariably present themselves in a highly complex context that we can only begin to unravel with appropriate tools of analysis at best.

Pieces of insight derived from the application of individual tools and techniques of analysis may also introduce error. Frameworks such as the "five forces" (Porter) model, for example, may have only limited applicability; a case in point is its applicability to the public services sector in which rivalry is essentially absent. Therefore, as a rule, all insights generated by individual frameworks need to be challenged for their underlying assumptions, verified and validated to the extent possible. This is particularly critical in the case of rapidly changing environments, where insights developed will have a very limited shelf life. In the final analysis, however, the ultimate usefulness of the framework is limited by our skill and ability to piece together the individual contributing elements of the analysis to construct a realistic representation of the "bigger picture" – one that enables better and improved strategic decision making.

STRATEGY IN PRACTICE: WHICH FRAMEWORKS?

Invariably the questions arise at the outset of a strategic analysis: *How many frameworks do I need to use? Which ones should I use? How do I best begin applying the frameworks?* These are valid questions; the following outline provides some broad guidelines for practice:

- Ultimately, the nature of the strategic question guides the choice of frameworks for the analysis; however, once the strategic question stands, it is important to begin with a suitable high-level framework of strategic analysis (such as the *opportunity–response* framework or the *unique competing space* framework, possibly even the *value proposition* framework) at the outset to guide the subsequent analysis.
- The high-level frameworks of strategic analysis guide the overall analysis; if appropriately selected they prompt and guide the application of suitable subordinate frameworks.
- Regardless of which of the three (or other suitable) high-level frameworks one selects, a robust strategic analysis invariably requires an analysis of (1) the organization's *external competitive environment*, (2) its *internal basis of competitiveness*, and (3) a verification of the organization's *strategic boundary conditions*.
- *External analysis:* The *PESTLE* framework is a suitable approach for initiating an external analysis. If done properly, it captures the relevant macroeconomic drivers and provides some indication of their dynamics. Subsequent

analyses might include a *key success factor* analysis indicating the prevailing "rules of the market place"; an assessment of the relevant industry sector's maturity with the help of an *S-curve* analysis. This can be followed up with an application of the *Porter "five forces"* analysis, which provides some insight into the nature of competition in that industry sector, and, finally, perhaps an analysis of the industry's *value chain* for evidence of the current value creation along that chain and some indication of its migration.

- *Internal analysis:* Frameworks such as a *resources and capabilities mapping*, followed up with *VRIO* (value, rare, imitable, organization) analysis represent suitable starting points for this analysis. This might be followed by an examination of the organization's *internal value chain* – and how it aligns with its *industry's value chain.*

- *Strategic boundary conditions:* An analysis of the organization's *value proposition* can produce substantial insight into the state of its strategic boundary conditions. For this, the outcomes of the foregoing external and internal analyses can be applied. An analysis of the organization's vision against the background of its guiding principles, aspirations and collective values completes the analysis of the value proposition.

- For the purpose of the foregoing analysis, we have used only a select few frameworks. Yet even on the basis of these few frameworks we can derive significant insight for strategic decision making – if the analysis is appropriately aligned with the relevant high-level strategic question.

SUMMARIZING THE CHAPTER . . .

- Supporting-level frameworks of analysis contribute depth and context to the "big picture" strategic mapping provided by the high-level analysis.

- Supporting-level frameworks of analysis provide insight regarding either external contexts or internal factors, not both.
- Supporting-level analyses are often limited by the validity and reliability of the data on which they are based. Hence, often the greatest benefit gained from their application is not the detailed output of the analysis, rather the structure their application contributes to the analysis and strategic thinking.
- While the insights contributed by individual supporting-level analyses can be useful, purposeful integration of contributions from a number of analyses can add immense richness to the overall insight to be gained from their application.
- Similarly, snap-shot (in time) analyses provide a first level of potentially useful insight; longitudinal analyses over time indicating trends can add significantly to the insight contributed by the analysis.

Notes

1. For example, www.valuebasedmanagement.net presents an exhaustive listing of management models; hyperlinks lead to a brief description of the model or framework in question.
2. See, for example: Grant, R.M. and Jordan, J. (2012) *Foundations of Strategy*, Chichester: John Wiley & Sons; Rothaermel, F.T. (2013) *Strategic Management*, New York: McGraw-Hill Irwin; or Gamble, J.E., Thompson, Jr., A.A. and Peteraf, M.A. (2013) *Essentials of Strategic Management*, 3rd ed., New York: McGraw-Hill Irwin.
3. Grant, R.M. (2010) *Contemporary Strategy Analysis*, 7th ed., Chichester: John Wiley & Sons.
4. Wheelen, T.L. and Hunger, J.D. (2012) *Concepts in Strategic Management and Business Policy*, 13th (International) ed., Upper Saddle River, NJ: Pearson.
5. Porter, M.E. (1980) *Competitive Strategy: Techniques for Analyzing Industries and Competitors*, New York: The Free Press.

6. Porter, M.E. (1985) *Competitive Advantage: Creating and Sustaining Superior Performance*, New York: The Free Press.
7. Rothaermel, F.T. and Hill, C.W.L. (2005) Technological Discontinuities and Complementary Assets: A Longitudinal Study of Industry and Firm Performance, *Organization Science*, Vol. 16, pp. 52–70.
8. Wernerfelt, B. (1984) The Resource-based View of the Firm, *Strategic Management Journal*, 5(2), pp. 171–180.
9. Barney, J.B. (1991) Firms' Resources and Sustained Competitive Advantage, *Journal of Management*, Vol. 17, pp. 99–120.
10. Peteraf, M.A. (1993) The Cornerstones of Competitive Advantage: A Resource-based View, *Strategic Management Journal*, Vol. 14, pp. 179–192.
11. Barney, J.B. and Hesterley, W.S. (2006) *Strategic Management and Competitive Advantage*, Upper Saddle River, NJ: Pearson–Prentice-Hall.
12. Barney, J.B. and Clark, D.N. (2007) *Resource-based Theory*, Oxford: Oxford University Press, pp. 69–71.
13. Grant, R.M. and Jordan, J. (2012) (note 2 above).
14. Prahalad, C.K. and Hamel, G. (1990) The Core Competence of the Corporation, *Harvard Business Review*, May–June; see also Hamel, G. and Prahalad, C.K. (1989) Strategic Intent, *Harvard Business Review*, May–June.
15. Leonard-Barton, D. (1995) *Wellsprings of Knowledge*, Boston: Harvard Business School Press.
16. Birchall, D.W. and Tovstiga, G. (2005) *Capabilities for Strategic Advantage – Leading through Technological Leadership*, Basingstoke: Palgrave Macmillan.
17. Helfat, C.E, Finkelstein, S., Mitchell, W., Peteraf, M.A., Singh, H., Teece, D.J. and Winter, S.G. (2007) *Dynamic Capabilities*, Oxford: Blackwell Publishing; see also Helfat, C.E. and Peteraf, M.A. (2009) Understanding Dynamic Capabilities: Progress Along a Developmental Path, *Strategic Organization*, Vol. 7, pp. 91.
18. Teece, D.J. (2009) *Dynamic Capabilities & Strategic Management*, Oxford: Oxford University Press.
19. For example, *Apple Inc.'s* market value on 18 July 2012 was US $538.35 billion; its book value on this date was US$109.63 billion. From this, a "Tobin's q" value of 5.53 can be calculated. Hence, the proportion of *Apple Inc.'s* market value attributable to intangible assets was 81.9% (source of data: http://finance.yahoo.com/q/ks?s=AAPL+Key+Statistics; accessed on 19 July 2012).

20. Adapted from Grant and Jordan (2012) (note 2 above).
21. Ibid.
22. Ibid.
23. The "iceberg" model is often attributed to Edgar H. Schein (1992) *Organizational Culture and Leadership*, 2nd ed., San Francisco: Jossey-Bass Publishers; Schein proposes three levels of the organization: (1) the visible part consisting of artifacts; (2) a lower level consisting of espoused values; and (3) an even lower, subconscious level comprised of basic underlying assumptions.

CHAPTER 7

Strategy Formation and Evaluation of Strategic Options

If you don't know where you are going, any road will get you there.

—Lewis Carroll (in *Alice in Wonderland*)

IN THIS CHAPTER, WE:

- examine how strategic analysis leads to a reconstructed "bigger picture" and then to the formation of strategic options;
- explore some simple mechanisms for strategy formation leading to the formulation of strategic options that relate to configurations of organizations determined by their maturity and dynamics of their competitive environment;

- examine three approaches for evaluating and scrutinizing the options derived for suitability on the basis of systematic frameworks.

With markets changing irreversibly, competition intensifying and businesses finding themselves suspended in between, managers are continually asking the same questions: What do we do next; where do we go from here? Which strategy will take us to where we wish to be? Do we reinforce our current competitive position; do we move into adjacent markers – or do we do something radically different?

In earlier chapters of this book we examined sense making and its role in the strategic thinking process as a prerequisite for strategic decision making. We saw that purposeful sense making begins with (1) the articulation of the relevant strategic questions and the framing of issues associated with these questions, (2) the deconstruction of the organization's complex reality, followed by (3) the reconstruction of reality through piecing together of the "big picture" with appropriate insight and intuition. In Chapter 5 we introduced two high-level frameworks of analysis, the *value proposition* and *unique competing space* frameworks that map the "big picture" reflecting the firm's competitive environment, both external and internal, with focus on the value offering that is at the core of an organization's strategic position.

In following through with the strategic thinking process to this point, where does this leave us? We now have the means for assembling the "bigger picture". The bigger picture, though inevitably incomplete, nonetheless reflects the current and relevant competitive landscape if prompted by the appropriate strategic questions. With the firm's reconstructed strategic landscape reflecting the firm's competitive position (Figure 7.1) now in place, we are in a position to begin with the formulation of strategic options. The preceding sense making guided by appropriate application of high-level strategic analysis provides the

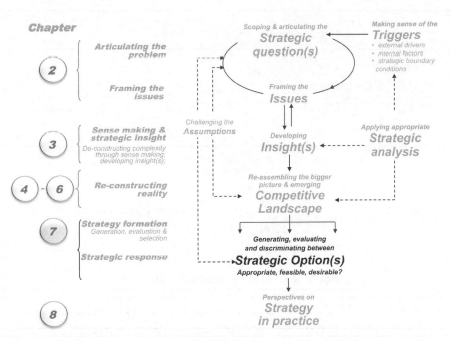

Figure 7.1 Strategy formation and the strategic option space

foundation on which we identify and derive suitable strategic options. From the options derived we seek one that enables an appropriate response to the strategic questions articulated at the outset. Clearly, the purpose of the strategic analysis, both high level and supporting level, is to guide our sense making in a direction that enables, ultimately, the selection of a strategic option that most suitably reflects the firm's positioning for creation and delivery of a (ideally, uniquely superior) value offering. In other words, the firm's strategic option space falls within the bounds of the firm's *unique competing space* (Figure 7.2).

Strategic options are not only bounded by the three boundaries of the firm's *unique competing space*, they are also subject to competitive conditions prevailing at those boundaries.

From the foregoing it would appear that the formation of strategic options is a straightforward procedure once the firm's *unique competing space* has been mapped. This is not the case, however,

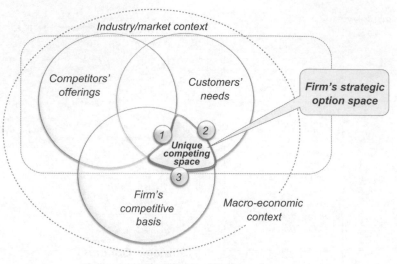

Figure 7.2 The firm's strategic option space

in practice. While it is true that good strategic analysis is an indispensable prerequisite for strategic option formation, a number of other factors play an important role; factors such as size, type and maturity of the organization. It is these factors that we examine in this chapter.

STRATEGY IN PRACTICE: STRATEGY FORMULATION IN ORGANIZATIONS

Even under the most favorable circumstances, however, the formulation of strategic options is not a trivial managerial task. It is subject to at least three complicating factors:[1]

- *Conditions of incomplete knowledge:* Organizations are complex. Knowledge within organizations is continually evolving and changing and is asymmetrically distributed; strategy formation therefore necessarily takes place under conditions of incomplete knowledge.
- *Power and conflicting interest:* Organizations embody political systems that feature actors of differing interests, differing power relations and legitimacy of claim to decision making. These may be conflicting and contradictory.

- *Ambiguity:* As a result of the foregoing factors, organizations feature varying degrees of ambiguity, some of which may be circumstantial, some of which may be deliberate.

Clearly, the three factors are not independent of one another. This adds to the complexity of strategic option formulation. It is against this backdrop that we now examine the next stage of the strategic thinking process – the formation and evaluation of suitable strategic options.

In the following two sections of this chapter we explore two aspects of strategy formulation. In the first section, we will examine how strategic options are formed. In the second section we then look at techniques for evaluating suitable options, and approaches for identifying and selecting from these one strategic option for execution.

Formation of Strategic Options

We find little consensus in the management literature on how strategy formation actually occurs in practice. While most strategists would agree that thorough analysis is a prerequisite for good strategy formation, there is no "one-scheme-fits-all" approach that we might fall back on for this step.

There is agreement, however, that not all strategies work equally well in every situation. Whether a firm selects a strategy of position, a strategy of leverage, or a strategy of opportunity comes down to its circumstances, its resource position and the disposition of its management.

Organizations, therefore, generally do not lock into any one particular mode of strategizing; nonetheless, precisely how strategies are formed remains a highly contentious debate.

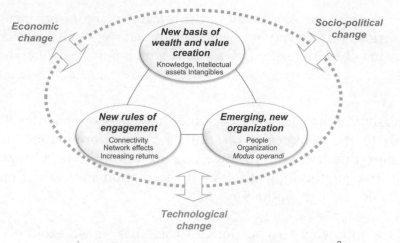

Figure 7.3 Emerging competitive organizational context[3]

Mintzberg[2] provokes a debate regarding the nature of strategy formation in practice and the validity of its representation in the strategic management literature that is perhaps long overdue. He argues that the strategy formation process might be far more devolved and nuanced than suggested in the current literature. The reasons for this lie in fundamental changes in the way in which organizations are conducting their business. There are a number of changes that are challenging prevailing conceptions of the role and functioning of organizations. Three major changes include the growing recognition of the importance of human capital, the empowering of the organization's knowledge workers, and new emerging forms of the organization as a competitive entity. These are portrayed in Figure 7.3.

We needn't look far to find evidence of the increasing importance and impact of the emerging new competitive entity suggested in Figure 7.3 in business practice.

New Basis of Wealth and Value Creation

Increasingly, wealth and value are finding expression in the form of intangible assets. One needs only to look at the development of firms' book value to their overall market capitalization. The "Tobin's q" ratio, which compares the market value of a company to its equity book value, has been discussed in Chapter 6. Understandably, the intangible part of a company's value is difficult to grasp, and even more difficult to "manage" in the traditional sense of the word. Yet this disproportionate part of firms' market capitalization captures much of the current irreversible trend underpinning the new basis of wealth creation.

Emerging, New Organizational Forms

New forms of the organization are emerging alongside the new forms of value and wealth creation. Partly, this is in response to the shifting competitive demands on organizations to become faster, nimbler and more agile. Partly, new forms are being driven by changing technological, economic and sociopolitical boundary conditions. For example, new generations of knowledge workers known as *digital nomads* are reshaping the traditional working places. Workplaces are evolving into knowledge market places. Market places generally share three common attributes: they involve an *exchange of goods*, a *transaction price* and *agents of the transaction*. In the emerging form of the organization, the goods of exchange are predominantly knowledge-related, the transaction price includes the package of negotiated terms of employment and the agents include both the knowledge worker and representatives of the organization.

New Rules of Engagement

Finally, we are finding new rules of engagement emerging within and between organizations. Increasingly, value and wealth creation are being driven by connectivity and network effects. Initially, these were enabled through technological advances, notably the Internet. Increasingly, though, they are being promulgated by economic and societal factors, such as social networks. In a business context, a *network effect* (sometimes also referred to as a network externality) represents the effect that one particular user of a good or service has on the value and impact that good or service has to other users. A *critical mass* triggering a *tipping point* situation (a point of no return that distinctly identifies a leading player) is achieved when the benefit or value derived from the good or service is greater than or equal to the price paid for it. Every new era heralds in new rules of engagement; those discussed here are particular to what we refer to as the *information* or *knowledge economy*.

The three factors described in the foregoing discussion (and possibly more) all stand to have an important impact on the way in which the nature of competition is changing irreversibly across industry and market sectors. The changing nature of competition in turn has an impact on firms' ability to compete. Firms are being forced to rethink their ability to compete. A firm's ability to compete and its competitive position, we have argued earlier, are reflected in its *unique competing space* for a given value offering. In particular, *change* in any of the determinants of the *unique competing space* – that is, change in the firm's *external context*, its *internal basis of competitiveness* and, consequently, the boundaries of its *unique competing space* – prompt the need for a strategic response on the part of the firm. The three factors depicted in Figure 7.3 all have implications for the determinants of a firm's unique competing space. Hence, an examination of any strategically relevant change is the logical point of departure for the formation of strategy.

The analyses we have examined in the preceding chapters – the analysis of the external context, the analysis of the firm's internal basis of competitiveness and its strategic boundary conditions – provide the basis upon which successful strategic options are derived and developed. Strategic options that emerge on the basis of these analyses and how they are derived depend on the specific competitive circumstances of the firm. The strategy formation process, with linkages to changes in the firm's competitive position, is depicted in Figure 7.4.

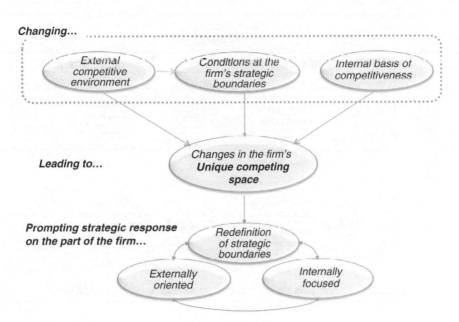

Changing...

External competitive environment

Conditions at the firm's strategic boundaries

Internal basis of competitiveness

Leading to...

Changes in the firm's **Unique competing space**

Prompting strategic response on the part of the firm...

Redefinition of strategic boundaries

Externally oriented

Internally focused

Figure 7.4 Strategy formation process

While we may not find a one-scheme-fits-all approach to strategy in the competitive context described earlier, we do find common patterns prevailing in strategy practice.

Different approaches for strategy formation emerge as a result of the specific strategic outcomes companies wish to achieve. Strategic options invariably fall into categories that reflect the firm's competitive context and strategic intent. These might include growth, but they might also include turnaround and retrenchment.

Mintzberg[2] categorizes firms in one of four distinct groupings or configurations suggested in Figure 7.5. Associated with these organizational types, we find organizational attributes or configurations that determine the primary mechanism for the strategy process in the respective organization.

1. *Institutionalized* (or "machine-type") organizations that rely primarily on a formalized *strategic planning process*.

Figure 7.5 Strategy formation; configuration and primary mechanisms.[2]

2. *Entrepreneurial-type* firms that rely on a *strategic visioning process*.
3. Firms in highly dynamic, emerging contexts (or *"adhocracy-type"* organizations) in which strategy formation is based on the *strategic learning process*.
4. *Professional-type* organizations that deploy *strategic venturing processes* for their strategy making

The attributes and mechanisms of strategy formation of each configuration are now examined in turn.

Strategy Formation in the Institutionalized Organization: Strategic Planning

These organizations are typically large, mature and are first and foremost focused on preserving the status quo, stability and predictability. Organizations of this form exhibit high levels of organizational inertia and are therefore resistant to internal change. They may even, if large, exert a stabilizing effect on their competitive environment. Internal stability is derived from a focus on standardized processes and efficiency of operations. With a strategic focus set on preservation, strategy formation is highly formalized and essentially consists of a strategic planning exercise that seeks to consolidate and institutionalize the strategic vision of the organization, an activity that is arguably more controlling than strategic in nature. Events prompting substantial change in strategy are interspersed with long periods of stability. Even in the event of change, it is less the organization as such than the form of the organization that changes. When facing a crisis, the institutionalized configuration may suspend its machine form and revert temporarily to the entrepreneurial form, enabling a strong leader to impose the required changes. This is what happened at *ABB*, the Swiss–Swedish engineering multinational, under Jürgen Dormann, who was brought in as CEO between September 2002 and December 2004 to get *ABB* back on track following its near collapse in late 2001. On adoption of the new strategic direction, however, the "turned around" organization typically reverts once more to its institutionalized form.

Strategy Formation in the Entrepreneurial Organization: Strategic Visioning

The strategy process is dominated by its leadership. This might be an individual; often the founder, though it might be a small team around the founder. The competitive context of the enterprise is more often than not highly dynamic. The enterprise typically is a small start-up or new entrant to an established market with a compelling new value offering. However, as described in the previous configuration, even a large institutionalized enterprise may go through punctuated periods or retrenchment or turnaround in which it most closely resembles the entrepreneurial configuration. The strategy process in this configuration therefore tends to be highly centralized and deliberately emergent in nature, reflecting on one hand the dynamic nature of the competitive environment and on the other the need for a clear strategy. This is often based on a novel vision for bringing the unique value offering to market – often product- or service-bound, but possibly via an innovative delivery mode. The entrepreneurial organization's leadership plays a central and direct role in the definition and enactment of its strategy.

Strategy Formation in Emerging, Dynamic Contexts ("Adhocracies"): Strategic Learning

These organizations are typically organized around teams of experts that are involved in project-type work. Often on the cutting edge of highly dynamic environments found in emerging technology or market contexts, strategy formation rests collectively with the teams of experts in these organizations. Their approach to strategy making might most appropriately be described as "flying by the seat of their pants". Strategy formation has a strongly emergent component; single projects – each representing a learning platform – establish precedents that nudge the organization toward new strategies through learning. The strategy process features a strongly collective learning-based component. This organization interacts closely with its competitive environment, alternatively taking the lead and receiving direction from the changing needs of its competitive environment. Periods of strategy convergence may follow on longer periods of divergence during which there is no apparent strategy due to the high degree of uncertainty in the external competitive environment. Indeed, the competitive environment tends to be more influential in strategy formation than any leadership role within the organization.

Strategy Formation in the Professional Organization: Strategic Venturing

The strategy process is influenced by the autonomous mode in which these individuals tend to interact; it is based on *strategic venturing*. Professional organizations consist of individuals loosely associated through a common organization. Individuals in these organizations are intent on pursuing their own professional interests, however, so that the strategy process tends to serve the needs of individuals more than it does those of the organization. The individuals' professional organizations have an important if indirect role in the strategy process as well; professional organizations are subject to standard practices and norms that are set by their respective professional governing bodies (e.g. medical boards or legal bar associations). Strategy process outcomes serve to ensure the continuity within relatively narrow limits of change in the value offerings of these organizations. Typically, these organizations provide professional standardized services in stable settings. The overall leadership impact on strategy formation in this configuration is weak relative to the other three configurations. Mintzberg compares the individual professionals in this configuration to "cats after their own prey, not easily herded". This pattern extends to the learning we find in the professional organization; we also find a dependence on learning. However, learning in the context of this organizational configuration focuses primarily on the learning of *individuals* in that organization, much as the loyalty of these individuals lies more with their professional peer group than with their organization.

Box 7.1 Europe's hidden champions

Family-owned firms in Europe have traditionally been safe havens in times of crisis. Many, after all, have legacies that span two world wars and numerous waves of nationalization. Family-owned or *Mittelstand* firms particularly dominate in Germany; a number of these have been described as *hidden champions*[4] by the German economist Hermann Simon. They exhibit traits of both institutional and entrepreneurial configurations. On the one hand they tend to be conservative and cautious; this expresses itself in their wariness of debt, easy money and speculation. On the other, family-owned firms intensely value honesty, careful work and nurturing close customer relations. They instill great loyalty in their workers. And they are largely successful: according to an index compiled by the Swiss bank *Credit Suisse*, family-owned firms have outperformed the *MSCI World Index* by 4.8% since its launch in 2007.

So, what is it that makes this hybrid configuration different? Europe's family-owned firms appear to succeed in combining the best of both the institutional and the entrepreneurial configuration attributes. Their low leverage, long-term approach and loyalty to their employees have not gone unnoticed in the wake of the current economic crisis. Most importantly, many firms in this sector are not subjected to the tyranny of quarterly reporting. A case in point is the German medical equipment producer *B. Braun Melsungen*, a family-owned firm that generated nearly €4 billion in sales last year. Equity makes up almost 40% of its balance sheet; yet despite profits of €185 million last year, less than 10% of that was paid out to its shareholders. There have even been some suggestions that this sector's approach to business could point the way to a more stable kind of capitalism.

However, some weaknesses have become apparent even in this sector. The first is that one of its strengths – the alignment of firm ownership and its management – can quickly become a liability when control is passed on to the next generation. Family-owned businesses also tend to lose caution when they get bigger. It seems that the less desirable attributes of the institutional configuration tend to hamper the performance of these firms, particularly as they are passed onto the following generation. Volker Beissenhirtz of *Schultze & Braun*, a German law firm, described the succession challenge facing these firms in the following way: "Sometimes they [the next generation management] are arrogant, sometimes they are naïve, sometimes they are really good, but they are never the original entrepreneur."[5]

Although presented as four distinct configurations earlier, Mintzberg's research provided evidence of a more complex situation concerning strategy formation. He found instances involving overlap and even infiltration of one configuration into another at certain points in an organization's development. This appears to be the case in which organizations evolve and develop over the course of their life-cycle.

Strategy Formation and Ambidexterity

The notion of ambidexterity in the context of strategic options prompts a dynamic view of strategy formation that positions configurations at various stages along the organizational life-cycle curve. Ambidexterity, a notion based on organizational design, reflects the ability of a firm to adapt in the face of change by simultaneous exploitation of its existing competitive position and exploration of new business opportunities; as such it represents a dynamic capability in the firm's portfolio of resources.[6] Shown in Figure 7.6, we find two main curves – one solid curve

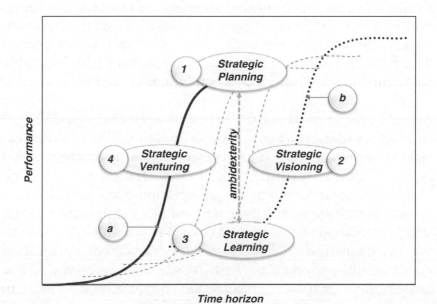

Figure 7.6 Primary mechanisms of strategy formation

representing the current business ("*a*"), and a second dotted one ("*b*") representing the "next curve", emerging business. Each curve represents a unique configuration consisting of a value proposition, business model and organizational attributes such as the organization's culture, paradigm and configuration of resources and capabilities. While the solid curve ("*a*") representing current, ongoing business is focused mostly on exploitation of current competitive opportunities that present themselves to the firm, the dotted curve ("*b*") represents an exploratory competitive stance on the part of the firm.

We find the four configurations proposed by Mintzberg situated on the two curves as depicted in Figure 7.6. The *strategic planning* focus of the *institutionalized* organizational configuration positions this organization at the top of the curve "*a*" at "*1*", which represents a mature stage of growth.

Positioned at "*2*" (Figure 7.6) on curve "*b*" we find the *entrepreneurial* configuration with its *strategic visioning* focus, while the *strategic learning* focus of the emerging, *ad hoc-type* configuration at point "*3*" is consistent with an early stage of growth. Finally, the *strategic venturing* orientation of the *professional* firm at "*4*" is positioned on curve "*a*" consistent with the stable environment described for this configuration earlier.

Arguably, the greatest polarity exists between configurations "*1*" and "*3*", spanning the two curves. Why is this? The two configurations represent two diametrically opposing organizational types. While the institutionalized configuration represents an entrenched position intent on preservation and exploitation of the current business, the emergent, ad hoc configuration represents exploration and disruption of the known. In Kelly's[7] terminology, the institutionalized (*exploitation*-oriented) organization is focused on "*perfecting the known*" while the emergent, ad hoc (*exploration*-oriented) organization typically seeks to "*imperfectly seizing the unknown*". The two configurations represent potentially contradictory organizational mindsets, cultures, processes and leadership challenges. Clearly, the two configurations have immense implications for the mode and nature of innovation pursued in the respective organizations. While the institutional configuration relies primarily on incremental innovation, the emergent form immerses itself in radical, frame-breaking innovation.

Few companies to date have demonstrated the ability to simultaneously pursue and balance *exploitation* and *exploration*; that is, to demonstrate *ambidexterity* by deriving competitive advantage from the current business while pioneering radical innovation to ensure the future. O'Reilly and Tushman[6] argue that an ambidextrous organization need not escape its past in order to renew itself for the future. The differences, however, are far from purely theoretical. Indeed, companies across all industry sectors are facing the challenges of bringing the two configurations under one hat. In the recent past, this has often resulted in failure. ABB, for example, in seeking to reposition itself from a purely "bricks and mortar" company to a globally competitive "clicks and mortar" player, established a corporate New Ventures Group in 2000 that was to forge closer links between "new economy" ventures (curve "*b*"-type businesses) and its traditional (curve "*a*") enterprise activities. The initiative, which was intended to serve as an innovation incubator to new, revolutionary business ideas, folded soon after its establishment. The newly established group proved to be incompatible with the established corporate environment; in ABB's context the differences in culture, objectives and the means to achieve these were insurmountable.

Today's global news media industry is facing similar challenges. Most daily newspapers around the world are engaged in a fight for their existence. A number of established newspapers were forced to close down their operations; the list of recent closures includes the *Baltimore Examiner*, *Cincinnati Post* and the *Halifax Daily News*. Expectations of free online content, a disruptive change to the traditional advertising business model and changes in the way people are accessing news have sent traditional newspapers around the world scrambling to experiment with ambidextrous business configurations that include traditional printed media alongside online editions. No newspaper appears to have resolved the problem successfully. Many are seeking organizational configurations that successfully bridge the gap between the traditional institutionalized and emergent business configurations. While the former delivers editorial comment, depth of analysis, printed content – and ever decreasing advertising revenues – the latter demands an entirely new business model that would ensure new streams of online advertising revenues. Needless to point out, the organizational demands, competencies and wherewithal of the two configurations couldn't be more different.

Strategy Formation: An Opportunity–Response Perspective

The *opportunity–response* analysis framework introduced in Chapter 5 provides an alternative dynamic perspective that can be used to visualize the outcome of a deliberate and purposeful response of the firm. Figure 7.7 indicates an alternative learning

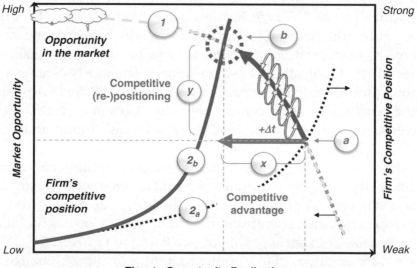

Figure 7.7   Strategic repositioning and in response to market opportunity

trajectory (labeled "2_b") representing the firm's accelerated learning trajectory that intersects the market opportunity curve at point "b" rather than at point "a". The accelerated learning trajectory results in both a lateral and vertical shift of the organization's competitive position relative to its original trajectory (curve "2_a", indicated with a broken line). The lateral shift depicted by a horizontal vector (origin at "a") represents the competitive advantage gained by an ability to deliver on the market opportunity sooner than originally targeted. The resulting competitive advantage (indicated by "x") is sometimes referred to as a *time-to-market* or *early-mover* advantage.

This advantage is measurable in ways that reflect the rewards early movers stand to reap. Achieving a time-to-market advantage is not to be underestimated. However, there is a second and often overlooked factor associated with first-mover advantage. This is indicated by the vertical shift (indicated by "y"). Inherent to the shift to an early-mover position is an internal repositioning of the organization's basis of competitiveness. An accelerated organizational learning curve that results in achieving early-mover advantage reflects deliberate effort on the part of the organization. This effort on the part of the firm is directed at transforming its competitive wherewithal – the configuration and exploitation of its strategic resources, capabilities, organizational culture and leadership.

Lastly, the transition along the market opportunity curve ("1") from points "a" to "b" (Figure 7.7) represents the range of strategic options deployed by the organization to achieve its accelerated competitive position. This might include internally focused organic growth, external growth through strategic partnering or perhaps even a combination of the two options.

The formation of strategy, as we have seen, requires a complex interplay of intuition and insight derived from experience, reflection and rational analysis, learning and visioning. Moreover, as we have seen in this section, the configuration of the organization reflecting its stage of growth and the competitive nature of its external competitive environment provide the specific context within which strategy formation occurs. What we have done in this section is to broadly scope the space within which strategy formation takes place. This field of study is still evolving. Indeed, as Mintzberg[2] suggests, many questions about how strategy formation happens in practice remain to be adequately resolved. In this section we have only scratched the surface. Hence, without any pretense of having dealt with the topic exhaustively, we will leave the topic of strategy formation on this note and move on to the final section in this chapter in which we examine how strategic options, once formulated, are appropriately evaluated and selected.

STRATEGY IN PRACTICE: STRATEGY FORMULATION – WHY BOTHER AT ALL?

The purpose of strategic analysis is to help the organization formulate strategic options for improving its competitive position through the creation and delivery of superior value to its stakeholders. Consequently, a lot of strategy is indeed formulated. The sobering fact, however, is that relatively little of the strategy formulated in organizations is actually put into practice. Estimates of strategies that fail to be put into practice range between 60 and 90%.[8] Now, there might be good reasons for this low estimation of strategies implemented: some of the strategies formulated in organizations are simply not good; they miss the mark, are unrealistic and therefore do not merit implementation in the first place. Rapidly changing competitive conditions make other strategies, possibly even good ones, prematurely obsolete. Alternatively, organizations find themselves incapable of putting potentially good strategies into practice due to internal factors that hinder their implementation.

Of course, very few CEOs would have the courage to stand up in front of their shareholders and the financial community and admit that only a fifth of their companies' formulated strategy has been put practice.

That is, until the recent economic crisis. The current economic climate has changed many things, including the attitudes of CEOs with regard to their strategies. More and more CEOs are showing a willingness to admit the inadequacy of their strategy in the current economic climate. Jamie Dimon, CEO of J.P. Morgan Chase & Co.,[9] admitted as much in late 2008 when suggesting that he had abandoned the organization's strategy projected for 2009 in view of the prevailing economic uncertainty.

Where does this leave strategy formulation? If anything, it suggests that increasingly even organizations of the *institutional* configuration are reverting to *adhocracy*-type strategy formation – strategy making of the type most suitable in dynamic and emerging competitive environments that exhibit ever shorter time horizons, and which draws heavily on organizational learning. Perhaps this is only a transitional phenomenon that we are observing. Perhaps not, though. There are indications suggesting that we are in the midst of an irreversible shift in the approach to strategy formation; that strategy formation will increasingly rely on an adhocracy-type approach, even in established enterprises.

Evaluation of Strategic Options

So, how do we proceed when we have succeeded in identifying and deriving a few potentially suitable strategic options? Strategic options invariably represent trade-offs and compromises – this is no more than a reflection of reality, which is complex and ever-changing. Hence, our evaluation of strategic options must necessarily take this into consideration: there is no such thing as a single right or wrong strategy in absolute terms.

How then is the evaluation of strategic options best approached in practice? There are several possible ways; we explore three approaches in this section, while noting that all target the same objective: to provide a systematic and structured evaluation framework that ultimately helps us to identify a preferred option from a set of several possible options. It is also important to note that the three approaches are not mutually exclusive; all share common elements.

Management Consulting Approach

Management consultancies tend to resort to decision tree-type algorithms or multiple criteria filters that subject the strategic options in question to a combination of quantitative and qualitative criteria that might include assessment of expected financial returns, achievement of strategic objectives, and level of risk. The objective of these approaches is to systematically compare options on the basis of both subjective and objective criteria. On this basis, the techniques deployed seek to screen out unsuitable options, ultimately leaving one option that best fulfills the criteria defined. There appears to be no limit to the sophistication built into the evaluation algorithms developed and deployed by some management consultancies. At the end of the day, however, even the most sophisticated technique is limited by the validity and reliability of the available data. Often, critical data required for a rigorous evaluation of strategic options is simply not available. In such cases, sophistication of technique offers no advantage over a well-balanced mix of good analysis and informed intuition. At worst, it bolsters a false sense of security "in the numbers", which, in fact, might consist of little more than "house numbers" in terms of relevance and validity.

Strategic Management Literature Approach

The strategic management literature suggests a number of evaluation schemes for scrutinizing strategic options once these have been derived. A number of textbooks on strategic management[10–13] propose algorithmic type frameworks that broadly seek to answer similar sets of questions concerning the strategic options under scrutiny listed in the following "Strategy in Practice" insert.

STRATEGY IN PRACTICE: DISCRIMINATING BETWEEN STRATEGIC OPTIONS

Generally, the questions that challenge the suitability of a strategic option fall into the following three categories:

- Is the strategic option *appropriate* – is the option consistent with the organization's available and needed resources, skills and competences, values and culture; is it simple and understandable?
- Is it *desirable* – does the option satisfy the objectives of the organization in terms of level of expected returns, synergies to be expected, level of risk it entails and stakeholder needs and expectations?
- Is it *feasible* – is the strategic option feasible in terms of the change that will be required; its ability to fulfill *key success factors*; the competitive advantage it promises to deliver and the demands on the organization for achieving this; its timing in relation to the opportunity it seeks to address?

The questions address three broad criteria categories, though in practice we might find overlap between these. Each category represents a cluster comprised of any number of sub-factors linked to the main criteria. These factors often entail detailed analyses, such as a *key success factor* analysis that provides insight on the feasibility of a particular strategic option.

Comprehensive Option Evaluation Framework Approach

A third approach (Figure 7.8) is based on a comprehensive framework that integrates elements of the strategic thinking process

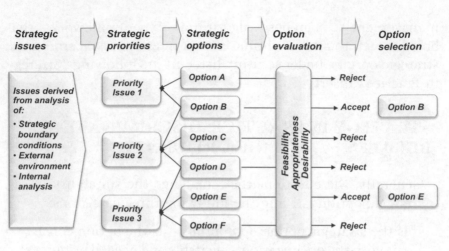

Figure 7.8 Strategic option evaluation framework[12]

introduced in the earlier chapters of this book and elements of the screening technique described in the previous section.

This approach begins with a strategic issues analysis, as described in Chapter 2. The issues are triggered by changes in the firm's competitive environment that give rise to the need for strategic action in the first place. The analysis of the issues and associated strategic questions culminate in a suitable prioritization. The high-priority issues and questions ultimately lead to the forma-tion of a range of options.

Following the example illustrated in Figure 7.8, the analysis has resulted in the determination of three priority issues. These are inevitably interrelated, giving rise to six strategic options. These six options are then subjected to a screening for suitability – defined broadly by *feasibility*, *appropriateness* and *desirability* with the help of a framework of the type described earlier in this section.

Once screened, we might find that only two of the original six options satisfy the *feasibility*, *appropriateness* and *desirability* criteria that have been defined within the specific strategic context of the company. These two might then be further screened in an additional iterative evaluation cycle. Alternatively, the final strategic option of choice might be a hybrid option comprised of elements of the two options that remain after a first pass of the evaluation.

STRATEGY IN PRACTICE: WHICH APPROACH TO STRATEGY EVALUATION AND SELECTION IS "BEST"?

We have presented only three approaches to strategy option evaluation, and even these share common elements. Which of the three is to be recommended? My personal preference is the last of the three discussed, the framework presented in Figure 7.8. This framework is most comprehensive and readily adaptable for application in a wide range of circumstances. Moreover, it draws on the strategic thinking process that forms the core theme of this book from the outset.

Finally, Some Caveats

The purpose of the evaluation process is to subject a set of strategic options derived from the strategic analysis to systematic and comprehensive scrutiny of criteria comprised of both objective and subjective components. The purpose of the evaluation frameworks is solely to provide structure to the thinking process, not to replace thinking. The outcome of the evaluation exercise will only be as good as the quality of the effort that has gone into it. This begins with the choice of the appropriate criteria for evaluation. The choice of balance between qualitative and quantitative evaluation inputs and their validity are further important factors; often reliable quantitative data simple isn't available, much as we tend to prefer "hard facts" for the sake of argumentation. Strategy is inherently about the future – any projection or extrapolation of data reflecting the organization's current situation into the future has a subjective character, even if numerically founded. Finally, when the evaluation has been completed, when a preferred option has been identified, we need to step back and critically do a final reality check by asking ourselves:

- Has the set of options considered for this evaluation been subjected to a sufficient number of the "right" criteria, for scrutiny; have "all the angles been covered" in the evaluation?
- What assumptions have gone into the evaluation; do they stand up to a reality check; which of them are the most critical for the analysis?
- How rigorous is the outcome; what are the uncertainties and risks?
- What are the potential "killer criteria"? Have these been clearly flagged; have they been appropriately weighted in the analysis?

SUMMARIZING THE CHAPTER . . .

- Strategies take shape in organizations on the basis of the "big picture" that emerges from strategic sense making and analysis.
- Strategic options present themselves within the bounds of the firm's *unique competing space*; they are influenced by competitive conditions prevailing at the boundaries of its *unique competing space*.
- Strategy formation occurs within a complex organizational context characterized by incomplete information, political interests and power, and ambiguity; there are no "hard and fast" approaches to strategy formation in organizations.
- Each context is unique and requires a unique approach. However, we do recognize that while we might not be able to describe strategy formation in detail, we can define broad parameters of the strategy formation space.

These relate to the maturity of the enterprise and the dynamics of its competitive context

- Strategic options, once derived, need to be scrutinized and evaluated for their feasibility, appropriateness and desirability; suitable criteria include both objective and subjective factors.
- Numerous approaches exist for doing this; three specific approaches are described in this chapter; the purpose of the evaluation is to identify from a set of options one that best fulfills the criteria imposed by the original strategic question that prompted the search for new strategic direction in the first place.
- Finally, we have seen that strategic options must be critically challenged on their underlying assumptions, their validity and suitability. It goes without saying that a suitable strategic option, once identified, has a shelf-life that is determined largely by the dynamics of the organization's competitive environment.

Notes

1. Wilson, D. (2003) Strategy as Decision Making, in Cummings, S. and Wilson, D. (eds) *Images of Strategy*, Oxford: Blackwell Publishing.
2. Mintzberg, H. (2009) *Tracking Strategies – Toward a General Theory*, Oxford: Oxford University Press.
3. Tovstiga, G. (2008) *Innovation Elective Lecture Script*, Henley Business School, University of Reading, UK.
4. Simon, H. (1996) *Hidden Champions*, Boston: Harvard Business School Press.
5. *The Economist* (2009) Dynasty and Durability (26 September 2009).
6. O'Reilly, C.A. and Tushman, M.L. (2004) The Ambidextrous Organization, *Harvard Business Review*, April, pp. 74–81; see also O'Reilly, C.A. and Tushman, M.L. (2008) Ambidexterity as a Dynamic Capability: Resolving the Innovator's Dilemma, *Research in Organizational Behavior*, 28, pp. 185–206.

7. Kelly, K. (1998) *New Rules for the New Economy*, New York: Viking.
8. Kaplan, R.S. and Norton, D.P. (2005) Creating the Office of Strategic Management, Working Paper No. 05-071, *Balanced Scorecard Collaborative, Inc.*
9. Colvin, G. (2009) How to Manage Your Business in a Recession, *FORTUNE European Edition* (26 January 2009).
10. Johnson, G.K., Scholes, K. and Whittington, R. (2008) *Exploring Corporate Strategy*, 8th ed., Harlow: FT Prentice Hall.
11. Thompson, J. with Martin, F. (2005) *Strategic Management*, 5th ed., London: Thomson.
12. Haberberg, A. and Rieple, A. (2008) *Strategic Management*, Oxford: Oxford University Press.
13. Mintzberg, H., Quinn, J.B. and Ghoshal, S. (1995) *The Strategy Process*, European Edition, London: Prentice Hall.

Insight-Driven Strategy in Perspective

There are those who make things happen; . . . there are those who watch things happen; . . . and then there are those who wonder what happened.

—Anonymous

IN THIS CHAPTER, WE:

- examine strategic thinking and insight-driven strategy from two practice perspectives:
  - a perspective set against the backdrop of complexity, uncertainty and multiple possible futures,
  - an organizational learning perspective;
- explore the implications of these perspectives in the context of how strategy is formulated and enacted in practice;
- examine strategy as a pretext for action and the creation of meaning in organizations;

- revisit the notion of organizational configuration introduced in the previous chapter and examine the implications of an organization's predisposition for how its
  strategy plays out in practice;
- conclude with a reflection on the purpose and implications of strategic thinking for strategy in practice.

So far we have examined how strategic thinking evolves from
the formulation of a compelling strategic question and a subsequent deconstruction of reality pertaining to that question
through an appropriate issues analysis. We have argued that
the need to revisit the firm's strategy at all is prompted by
changes to its *unique competing space* and, in particular, perturbations at the boundaries of that domain. We saw how
insights are derived on the basis of analysis and intuition in
response to the issues, and how these collectively contribute to
a reconstruction of the bigger picture that, even if incomplete,
nonetheless reflects the competitive context of the firm. Strategic thinking, we have argued all along, serves ultimately to
help us identify a viable strategy in response to the strategic
question that triggered the whole exercise in the first place (as
depicted in Figure 8.1). The underlying premise throughout this
book has been that a firm needs a strategy; that strategy formation is a necessary endeavor of the firm in moving forward. But is
this unequivocally so?

Some strategy thinkers have challenged this notion. De Bono's[1]
assertion that "strategy is good luck rationalized in hindsight",
or Burgelman's[2] claim that "strategy is a theory about the
reasons for past and current success of the firm" are examples.
These statements suggest that what we call "strategy" is often
really only a retrospective summary of action that lies in the
past. The bias we exhibit in hindsight, the apparent coherence
and rationality of the strategy in question might therefore
actually result in misleading conclusions in respect of what
we can do now and what we need to do in the future.[3] Indeed,

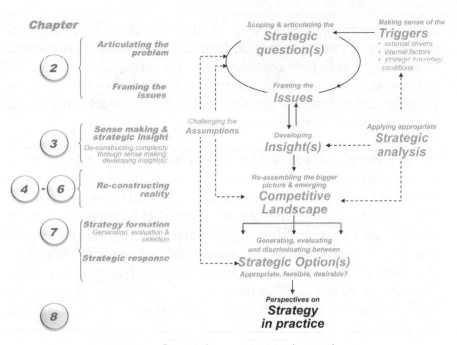

Figure 8.1 Perspectives on strategy in practice

Mintzberg *et al.*[4] have argued that a lack of strategy is sometimes even desirable, especially when in transition between an outdated one and a new, more viable one – or when environments are so dynamic that it makes sense to temporarily suspend all pretense of a strategy until the environment settles down somewhat. J.P. Morgan Chase & Co. CEO Jamie Dimon's exclamation in late 2008: *"I am shocked by the number of people who are still worrying about their strategic plan for 2009. We cancelled all that stuff – all of it"*[5] is a statement to that effect.

Where does this leave the strategic thinking process? Complex and turbulent competitive contexts do not preclude the need for strategic thinking. Strategic thinking under these circumstances may, indeed, even lead to a temporary suspension of a strategy – as suggested by J.P. Morgan Chase's Dimon. If at all, circumstances experienced by business managers today demand a better understanding of the greater context within which strategy occurs in practice, in real organizations. Not only is that context becoming increasingly complex, it is the emerging management practice field within which strategy and strategic thinking occur. It is the organizational context that ultimately determines the appropriateness of any strategy effort.

In the previous chapter we have examined strategy formation in a variety of contexts determined by the dynamics in the enterprise's external competitive environment and its stage of maturity. In this closing chapter we extend this view to explore strategy and strategic thinking as such in an evolving environment that is increasingly unpredictable and complex. We close the chapter with a look at emerging organizational practices that are supportive of strategy and the strategic thinking in today's complex though nonetheless real competitive business environment.

Strategy in practice – the way strategy plays out in the reality of an organization's context – can be examined from multiple perspectives. We restrict ourselves to examining only two in this chapter. We begin with an external perspective. In view of the current global economic recession such a perspective is rather timely. Many companies are currently struggling to come to grips with the implications of the crisis for their strategy. The external perspective we will examine is one prompted by multiple possible futures.

For the second perspective we delve into the organization and explore strategy practice from an internal organizational perspective. Specifically, we look at the learning organization. Why these two perspectives? They represent two different views – one externally instigated; the other relating to internal determinants. Arguably, these two perspectives aptly reflect many of the key factors that are prompting changes in management thinking in the field of strategy today.

Multiple Possible Futures Perspective

As our emerging global economy is expanding in the wake of unprecedented technological and socioeconomic change, it is increasingly ushering in its own new rules and distinct opportunities. All the while, it is relegating to obsolescence traditional and existing approaches to management theory that view the world as predictable, linear, measurable and controllable.

The emerging competitive landscape is complex; it is comprised of a context involving emerging patterns of behavior of organizations, market places, economies and political infrastructures.[6] One of the implications for organizations emerging from this reality is that of multiple possible futures with varying degrees of uncertainty. Courtney[7] has suggested four possible futures and implications for strategy under the respective circumstances:

- *Level one: Single view of the future* – emerging from a relatively stable environment with a high degree of predictability and little uncertainty.
- *Level two: Limited set of possible futures* – one of which can be expected to occur with high probability.
- *Level three: Range of possible future outcomes* – with increasing uncertainty as to the outcome most likely to occur.
- *Level four: Limitless range of possible future outcomes* – with any outcome possible.

Courtney argues that while all four situations have always existed, a lot more of these are of the *level three* and *level four* type than we would previously have thought to be the case.

What does this situation entail for strategy and strategic thinking? *Level one* through *level three* situations can be bounded in terms of possible outcomes; with uncertainty obviously increasing with each level. Nonetheless, in all three cases some analysis is possible. Key drivers and triggers can be identified; some analysis of the external environment and the internal context are possible, though with each increasing level the dynamics of the external environment renders this ever more difficult. While a precise forecast may not be possible, approximate bounds of the possible outcomes can be staked out.

Level four situations, on the other hand, represent those for which the range of possible outcomes cannot be bounded. The distant future is fundamentally "unknowable"; it's a situation in which anyone's guess goes. Does this mean that none of what we have examined in previous chapters can be applied? Are companies in these circumstances left simply with the option to "wing it"?

Not at all. *Level four* situations do not eliminate the need for rigorous strategic thinking. However, this level of uncertainty does require a different mindset. *Level four* requires an exploratory mindset of the type encountered in the emergent, *adhocracy*-type organizational configuration examined in the previous chapter. We also saw that *strategic learning* served as the primary strategy process in this type of organization. Indeed, strategic learning is not only called for in *level four* situations; in view of the evolving dynamics of change in global competitive environments, strategic learning is becoming indispensable for the strategy process at all levels.

So, what insights does this perspective contribute to our discussion? First, it suggests plausible boundaries to the type of strategy making firms are likely to be engaging in. In our current economic climate, few firms are enjoying the luxury of *level one* and *two* contexts; most are facing *level three* and *four* situations. However, their competitors are in the same situation. So, while this doesn't mean that strategy should be approached any less rigorously, it does mean that companies need to approach strategy *differently*. Embedding a strategic learning perspective is one way of achieving this objective.

Organizational Learning Perspective

The strategic thinking process features all the components of a classic learning process. Hence it is appropriate that we close the final chapter of this book with a brief reflection on the learning perspective in strategy. It is not by chance that the strategic learning perspective has attained disproportionate attention in recent years. It is arguably the most amenable to building a position of sustainable competitive advantage in today's turbulent business environment. In practice it finds expression in the learning organization and integrates elements of the emergent strategy school. However, as Mintzberg[8] points out, every sensible real-life strategy necessarily combines emergent learning with some degree of deliberate control on the part of the firm's management. Strategy in this context has been described in various ways – as encouraging open communication, with a bias for experimentation and reflection, whereby learning through trial and error is tolerated, perhaps even deliberately fostered by management. Indeed, the learning organization is in many ways the antithesis of the traditional, bureaucratic, institutionalized organization which would be operating primarily in a controlling mode.[9]

STRATEGY IN PRACTICE: STRATEGY AND ORGANIZATIONAL LEARNING

It is difficult to imagine an organization devoid of any learning. Senge[10] describes two types of organizational learning, both of which are critical for the strategy process, albeit in different ways:

- *Adaptive reactive learning:* This entails reacting to impulses from the external competitive environment.
- *Generative learning:* This form of organizational learning is pre-emptive and geared towards anticipating the future environment.

The two learning modes are positioned between two extremes of the spectrum of management styles. These have been described in Chapter 7 (depicted in Figure 7.5) as the two diametrically opposed organizational configurations – the *institutionalized* configuration and the *emerging, adaptive configuration. Adaptive learning* is typically found in institutionalized organizational configurations while *generative learning* is the mode most amenable to an emerging, adhocracy-type configuration.[11] It is to be assumed that increasingly, *generative learning* will be the preferred mode of learning adopted by organizations.

The two extreme organizational learning styles (*adaptive* versus *generative*) are aptly described in the following quotation, which has been attributed to Stacey:[12]

> **Ordinary management** *is practiced when most of the managers in an organization share the same mental models or paradigm. Cognitive feedback loops then operate in a negative feedback manner so that shared mental models are not questioned; ordinary management is about rational processes to secure harmony, fit, or convergence to a configuration, and it proceeds in an incremental manner.*

> **Extraordinary management** *involves questioning and shattering paradigms, and then creating new ones. It is a process which depends critically upon contradiction and tension . . . Extraordinary management, then, is the use of intuitive, political, group learning modes of decision making and self organizing forms of control in open-ended change situations. It is the form of management that managers must use if they are to change strategic direction and innovate.*

We have already argued in Chapter 7 that the two management styles and associated organizational configurations have important implications for the strategy process. Firm's predispositions have a direct bearing on the approach to strategy taken. Their respective predisposition is embedded in their fundamental organizational configuration – their structure, processes, culture and leadership. Increasingly, Stacey's notion of *extraordinary management* is becoming the predisposition of firms focused on achieving a sustainable position of competitive advantage.

Box 8.1 Strategic Dissonance and Strategic Inflection Points

An anecdote recounted by former Intel Chairman and CEO Andy Grove[13] provides an apt example of *extraordinary management*. In reflecting on Intel's exodus from the memory chip business in the mid-eighties, in which it had at one point held practically a 100% share of the market, to the microprocessor business, Grove refers to the *strategic dissonance* and *strategic inflection points* Intel experienced in the critical years in which it abandoned the memory chip business and established itself as market leader in the microprocessor business.

What had happened? Intel as first mover had developed and introduced memory chips or "memories" to the nascent computer industry soon after its start-up in 1968. Competitors, mostly American and small in size, followed in the early seventies. Throughout the seventies competition for the next generation of memory chips was largely among American companies. During this period, Intel kept its leadership position. Then, in the early eighties, the Japanese made their appearance in force in the memory chip market. Not only did they rapidly build an awesome capacity base in memory chip manufacturing, but the quality levels of Japanese memories were consistently and substantially better than those produced by American companies. In fact, Japanese quality levels were superior to what was thought possible by Intel. What exacerbated the situation for Intel was not only that the Japanese offered superior quality, but that they did so at market dumping price levels. All the while Intel continued to spend heavily on research and development. It focused mostly on improving its memory chips, but some R&D effort was also devoted to a new technology for another device that had been invented in the early seventies: microprocessors. Both microprocessors and memories are built with a similar silicon chip technology, but their design is different. Microprocessors calculate; they are the brains of the computer while memory chips merely store information. Because they represented a slower-growing and smaller-volume market than memory chips their technology development was not considered a priority.

That changed after 1984 when memory chip sales virtually collapsed. Intel lost their bearings and was floundering. Its priorities and identity were clearly still focused on memories. In fact, the importance of memories to Intel was firmly embedded in its very beliefs and corporate dogma. Yet memories had become a worldwide commodity. Intel was at a loss as to what to do. In Grove's words, Intel entered into a period of *strategic dissonance* – a period marked by divergence between an organization's actions and its statements. This was a critical three-year period in which Intel's middle management were already in the process of positioning the company in the emerging microprocessor market while its senior management was still engaging in heated strategy debates on how to recapture its former leading position in the memory chip market.

Grove recalls asking Intel's chairman and CEO, Gordon Moore, in a meeting sometime in mid-1985: "*If we got kicked out and the board brought in a new CEO, what do you think he would do?*" To which Gordon responded without hesitation: "*He would get out of memories.*" Grove, staring at him numbly, countered: *"Why shouldn't you and I walk out the door, come back and do it ourselves?"*

The rest, as they say, is Intel history. Fortunately, the adjustment of Intel's strategic posture from manufacturer of memories to manufacturer of microprocessors had already begun some time before Intel's senior management caught on. While its senior management was still looking for clever memory strategies men and women lower in Intel's organization were already initiating the change in direction. Increasingly, production resources were being directed to the emerging microprocessor business – not as a result of senior management direction, but rather as a result of daily decisions by middle managers close to the business front in the face of declining demand for memories and increasing opportunities for business profitability from microprocessors. By the time that Intel's senior management made the formal decision to exit the memory business, only one out of eight silicon fabrication plants were producing memories. The change in strategic direction – in Grove's terminology, Intel's *strategic inflection point* – took a total of three years. It turned out that the exit decision had a significantly less drastic market impact than anticipated and feared by Intel's senior management. A typical reaction of Intel's customers on being informed about Intel's decision to exit memories was: *"It sure took you a long time."*

Grove draws a number of important lessons from Intel's strategic transition period relevant to the strategic learning perspective.

One of these lessons concerns the immense immobilizing effect that a firm's identity can have. In Intel's case, its legacy and identification with memories formed one of its deep corporate beliefs that, by Grove's admission, were as strong as religious dogma. These blocked the way for an open-minded and rational discussion during the crucial period in which Intel's memory chip markets were rapidly eroding. Interestingly, Intel's customers, having no emotional stake in Intel's decision-making process, had far less difficulty in realizing much sooner what Intel should have been doing. New managers are also often much less encumbered by *legacy thinking* – the emotional involvement experienced by people who have devoted long periods of their life to a company, and who are typically incapable of applying impersonal logic to a situation that calls for detached reasoning.

Finally, it is usually the "people in the trenches" who are in touch with impending changes and the need for strategic adjustment much earlier than senior management. Grove emphasizes this point by pointing out that:

While management was kept from responding by beliefs that were shaped by our earlier successes, our production planners and financial analysts dealt with allocations and numbers in an objective world. For us senior managers, it took the crisis of an economic cycle and the sight of unrelenting red ink before we could summon up the gumption needed to execute a dramatic departure from our past.[13]

Intel's strategy shift is remarkable for several reasons. First, it is an example of a successful organizational transformation that was primarily grassroots-driven. Second, it resonates with what has always distinguished great strategy in military contexts: the ability, when necessary, to drop preconceived notions and adapt action in accordance with present circumstances. Greene[14] argues that the greatest generals stand out not because they have more knowledge but because of their ability to change a course of action in the face of changing circumstances. Greene elaborates that knowledge, experience and theory have limitations in that no amount of advance thinking can prepare you for the ambiguity and countless possibilities often presented in critical circumstances. The Prussian military theorist Carl von Clausewitz referred to the difference between plan and actual happening as *friction*; it is what Grove has called *strategic dissonance.* Since *friction* or *strategic dissonance* are inevitable in reality, the better we are at adapting our thinking to changing and new circumstances, the more appropriate our responses to those changes will be. Conversely, the more we cling to obsolete and legacy thinking, the more inappropriate the response.

In many ways, Intel's experience confirms Weick's[3] assertion that "execution is [strategic] analysis and implementation is [strategy] formulation". Indeed, organizational configuration is an important factor in determining the approach taken by firms in "finding their strategy". Recall the diametrically opposing configurations discussed in Chapter 7. On one hand, the institutionalized configuration representing an entrenched position focused on preservation and exploitation of the current business (*"perfecting the known"*); on the other, the emergent and ad hoc organizational configuration intent on *"imperfectly seizing the unknown"*.[15] Intel's period of *strategic dissonance* represents a case illustration of the tension organizations experience when positioned between the two configurations. Not all organizations, however, succeed in resolving the dilemma as well as Intel did. The list of companies that struggled until their final demise to "perfect the known" is long. One needs only to look at companies that have been bumped off the *Fortune 100* list over the years for evidence of this.

Weick[3] argues that what is more important than an *a priori* deliberate strategy is a mechanism for channeling and stimulating focused and intense action. This in turn creates meaning and provides the requisite stability and structure for the organization to "get on with it" in the absence of a strategic rationale. Even a vague plan, map or explanation can serve the purpose. More important than the coherence and accuracy of the plan is the response and attention it receives from the organization. Meaning and validation of the emerging strategic direction then often only take shape *ex tempore*.

To illustrate this point Weick cites the example of the Naskapi natives of Labrador. The Naskapi employ an unusual approach to deciding where they should hunt. A shoulder bone of a caribou is held over a fire until it begins to fracture. The natives take direction on where to hunt from the cracks in the fractured caribou shoulder. Surprisingly, this approach appears to work well for the Naskapi; they almost always succeed in finding game.

Weick offers possible explanations for why this approach appears to work for the Naskapi: the natives end up spending most of each day hunting once they have taken direction from the fractures in the caribou bone. They don't sit around the fire debating on where they should be hunting. On those rare days on which they do fail to find game there is no individual to blame. The failed effort is attributed to the gods testing their faith. The fractured caribou bone keeps the Naskapi moving; by their very action the amount of insight multiplies the data from which meaning can be derived.

Strategy thus often becomes apparent only through retrospective reflection. The coherence and rationality of strategy often become inflated by bias introduced in hindsight. This can lead to misleading conclusions on what needs to be done currently and what appropriate action should be taken in future.

Does this refute the strategic thinking approach encompassing both analysis and intuition that has been the fundamental premise in this book? Not at all. As argued earlier, strategic thinking is an activity, of which the outcome might vary considerably. Ultimately, the outcome reflects the quality of the thinking that has occurred. Key to good strategic thinking is a clear understanding of the limitations of the insights generated at any point in time. Situations requiring action evolve even as we are required to act. Hence the centrality of the learning process in strategy; learning in the guise of action from which experience and meaning are derived. This is the essence of strategy in practice.

Sutton[16] has looked at how organizations can promote learning cultures. He suggests encouraging approaches and practices that run countercurrent to the prevailing business logic in order to maximize the learning essential for survival in today's relentlessly changing competitive environments. In essence his approach might be seen as a modern business version of the Naskapi caribou bone technique.

An extract from Sutton's list of suggestions for breaking the stranglehold of institutionalized logic is presented in the following summary.

STRATEGY IN PRACTICE: BREAKING THE STRANGLEHOLD OF INSTITUTIONALIZED LOGIC

- In approaching a problem or a new situation emerging from changing circumstances, don't study how a problem of this kind has been approached in the company, industry or field where you are working – learn to forget by discarding old ways and bringing in people who never knew about the good old days.
- If you do happen to know a lot about how a problem of the type has been resolved previously, bring people on board who are ignorant of it to study it and help resolve it – include a few crackpots, heretics and dreamers, especially if they are wildly optimistic about their ideas.
- Go outside of your industry for fresh ideas; study how analogous problems have been resolved elsewhere.
- To remind people about the dangers of taken-for-granted assumptions, revisit ideas that were proposed in your company and elsewhere that were once thought to be absurd, but are now widely accepted.
- Identify the most absurd things that companies in other industries are doing (or have done), and develop arguments about why your company ought to do them.
- Use a devil's advocate and dialectical inquiry: assign people to challenge your group's assumptions and

decisions and to develop arguments that the opposite assumptions and decisions are actually superior.

- Encourage people to be agnostic about the best business models, business practices and technologies.
- Hire and retain slow learners of the organizational code.
- Recall the past in your company and others, but interpret it as a cautionary tale about all the blunders and failures suffered by those who become snared in success traps.
- Encourage people to keep fighting over whether established practices are obsolete.

In essence, we conclude that insight-driven strategy is most aptly practiced and most likely to yield strategically relevant insights in an organizational context most closely resembling that of a learning organization. It is in this context that we find organizations capable of the cumulative learning and continual self-renewal required for sustainable competitive positioning.

STRATEGY IN PRACTICE: ADOPTING AN APPROPRIATE LEARNING MINDSET

Lampel[9] describes learning organizations as those that:

- Can learn as much, if not more, from failure as from success;
- Reject the adage *"if it ain't broke, don't fix it"*;
- Assume that the managers and workers closest to the core of the business, whether this be in design, manufacturing, distribution, or the sale of the product, often know more about these activities than their superiors;
- Actively seek to move knowledge from one part of the organization to another, to ensure that relevant knowledge ends up in the organization where it is most needed;
- Invest a lot of effort looking outside their own organization for knowledge.

A Closing Reflection on Insight-Driven Strategy in Practice

In previous discussions we have examined perspectives on how strategy plays out in practice. The choice of the term "plays out" is deliberate, since we might justifiably ask ourselves how much of strategy is deliberately decision-driven and how much of strategy is recognizable as a pattern only after the fact. And in light of this, one might ask: Where does strategic thinking fit into all of this?

It would appear that increasingly strategy thinkers are reluctant to view strategy as deliberate decision making, as intended by the plan. Increasingly, strategy is seen as a "pattern in a stream of decisions" manifested, though, in concrete actions.[8] Decisions, though implied by the actions, are much more elusive. If decision does indeed precede action then the evidence of its realization might range from a statement of intent to nothing at all. Viewing strategy as a stream of actions challenges earlier implicit assumptions made in the literature of organizational theory which suggests that decision precedes action. Mintzberg's[8] view of strategy, positioned along the continuum between deliberate and emergent – though with an important learning component that resonates more strongly with the emergent view – is consistent with that of Weick,[3] one of the few organizational thinkers to have suggested this early on and, moreover, to have suggested that this need not necessarily be a cause for managerial concern. In fact, he argues that deliberate "strategy" can hurt an organization, possibly leading to paralysis, and that strategy-like outcomes can originate from sources other than deliberate strategy. Weick proposes three themes that suggest how strategy plays out in practice: (1) that action gives rise to, and clarifies, meaning; (2) that the pretext for action is of secondary importance; and (3) that deliberate strategic planning is only one of many pretexts for the generation of meaning in organizations. Weick (2001) recounts the following anecdote (Box 8.2), an incident that allegedly occurred in the Great War, to illustrate his interpretation of strategy.

BOX 8.2 ALPINE EXCURSION

A small Hungarian military unit on a reconnaissance mission in the Swiss Alps lost their way in an intense snow storm that lasted for two days. The young lieutenant who had sent out the unit, fearing that he had dispatched the unit to their certain death, was devastated after the unit failed to show up by the second day. However, on the third day the unit returned unscathed and in good spirits. What had transpired? How had they found their way back? Members of the unit recounted how they had indeed considered themselves lost until one of the soldiers in the unit found a map in his pocket. That inspired confidence and prompted the unit to pitch camp and to sit out the storm in the relative safety of their tents. After the storm had broken, they had determined their bearings with the help of the map and proceeded to make their way back to the base camp.

The lieutenant asked to borrow the map and closely examined it. To his astonishment he realized that it was not a map of the Alps at all, but of the Pyrenees!

Did it matter to the lost reconnaissance unit? Not at all, as it turned out. Conceivably, though, it might well have – though detrimentally – had the soldiers realized that it was map of the Pyrenees. As it happened, the discovery of the map strengthened their resolve to survive, mobilized clarity of thinking and prompted focused action. Thereby, irrational though it might seem in hindsight, an entirely irrelevant map saved the unit from almost certain death in the icy alpine wilderness.

Is the insight-driven approach to strategy, indeed is *strategic thinking*, inconsistent in view of the positions argued by Mintzberg and Weick? Not at all. Savvy strategic thinking, by virtue of its facility to animate and orient people in organizations, is entirely consistent with Weick's notion of strategy in practice: people acting, learning and thereby creating meaning, even if in the absence of a rigorous rationale. These are what enable an appropriate strategic response. Weick's anecdote about the lost alpine reconnaissance unit underscores this point. The map, despite its factual irrelevance, achieved the following: its discovery restored the unit's confidence; it prompted action that enabled the soldiers to survive the storm. And when that had broken, it got them moving in some general direction. Once on the move, iterative observation and reflection enabled the unit to assess where they were in relation to where they wanted to go. Meaning was thereby derived from the circumstances as they evolved – these ultimately led the unit back to their base camp.

What then were the elements of the "strategy" that brought the reconnaissance unit safely back to their base camp; what were its elements? First, it was the action that gave rise to meaning; second, the map as pretext for that action was only of secondary importance; and third, deliberate "strategic planning" as such might be argued to have been inapplicable in this case altogether considering that the map was factually irrelevant to the circumstances.

Strategy as a pretext under which people act and generate meaning in response to changing circumstances is often only recognized as such in retrospect. Given the nature of the complex and fast-changing context of our competitive environments today, regardless of industry, this is a realistic assessment. In a way, this perspective on strategy should not surprise. It is intrinsically Darwinian. Already Darwin understood why adaptation is often so much more powerful than the setting of deliberate direction in the face of evolutionary change. Business environments resemble evolving ecosystems much more than they do the static and predictable settings often assumed in strategic analysis.

This take on reality, however, need not imply chaos and infer helplessness. However, strategic pretexts for action do need to derive contributions from a balance of clear intentions and action based on the best analysis available *and* from action and occurrences that were entirely unplanned for. Further, allowance must be for the fact that plans may not result in outcomes in the way originally intended. Strategic intent and evolving reality thus become much more entwined as action is taken and the firm observes and reflects on what works and what doesn't – and from this derives further appropriate action to be taken.

Strategic thinking might be viewed as an integral component in the strategy process in practice that underpins this activity; it serves as a guiding mechanism for analysis, intuition and interpretation in the creation of meaning, thereby enabling the derivation of insight required for appropriate strategic action.

SUMMARIZING THE CHAPTER . . .

- Strategy, though invariably instigated by external factors, is ultimately a pretext for organizational response.
- Strategy as a pretext for response in practice occurs along a continuum of activities positioned between those that are a result of deliberate control and those that are purely emergent in nature.
- Strategy more often than not is recognizable only in hindsight; its coherence and rationality discernible only *a posteriori*.
- Strategy in practice is therefore perhaps most aptly viewed as a pretext for action, from which meaning is derived only after the fact.
- Strategy in practice derives direction from deliberate planning as much as it does from unintended occurrences and actions.
- Whether through its contributions to rational analysis, intuition or interpretation thereby leading to the

ascription of meaning in retrospect, strategic thinking plays a critical role regardless of where we are along the strategy continuum.

Notes

1. DeBono, E. (1984) *Tactics: The Art and Science of Success*, Boston: Little, Brown.
2. Burgelman, R.A. (1983) A Model of the Interaction of Strategic Behaviour, Corporate Context, and the Concept of Strategy, *Academy of Management Review*, 8, pp. 61–70.
3. Weick, K. (2001) *Making Sense of the Organization*, Oxford: Blackwell Publishing.
4. Mintzberg, H., Ahlstrand, B. and Lampel, J. (2005) *Strategy Bites Back*, Harlow: FT Prentice Hall.
5. Colvin, G. (2009) How to Manage Your Business in a Recession, *FORTUNE European Edition* (26 January 2009).
6. Boulton, J. and Allen, P. (2007) Complexity Perspective, in Jenkins, M., Ambrosini, V. and Collier, N. (eds) *Advanced Strategic Management*, 2nd ed., Basingstoke: Palgrave Macmillan.
7. Courtney, H. (2008) A Fresh Look at Strategy under Uncertainty: An Interview, *The McKinsey Quarterly*, December 2008.
8. Mintzberg, H. (2009) *Tracking Strategies*, Oxford: Oxford University Press.
9. Lampel, J. (1998) Towards the Learning Organization, in Mintzberg, H., Ahlstrand, B. and Lampel, J. (eds) *The Strategy Safari*, New York: The Free Press.
10. Senge, P.M. (1990) The Leader's New Work: Building Learning Organizations, *Sloan Management Review*, Fall, pp. 7–23.
11. Hall, R. (1997) Complex Systems, Complex Learning, and Competence Building, in Sanchez, R. and Heene, A. (eds) *Strategic Learning and Knowledge Management*, Chichester: John Wiley & Sons, Ltd, p. 53.
12. Hall, R. (1997) Note that this quotation is taken from Hall (1997) – which attributes the quotation to Stacey (1993); (Stacey, R.D. (1993) *Strategic Management and Organisational Dynamics*, Pitman) – although the quotation appears not to have made it into R.D. Stacey's 4th edition (2003) of the book.

13. Grove, A. (1996) *Only the Paranoid Survive*, New York: Currency Doubleday.
14. Greene, R. (2006) *The 33 Strategies of War*, London: Profile Books, pp. 21–22.
15. Kelly, K. (1998) *New Rules for the New Economy*, New York: Viking.
16. Sutton, R.I. (2002) *Weird Ideas that Work*, New York: The Free Press.

Putting Strategy to Practice

Probing the Strategic Boundaries of the Firm's Unique Competing Space

IN APPENDIX 'A' WE:

- derive practical guiding questions for reflecting on the dynamics and their strategic implications at the boundaries of the firm's unique competing space
- provide templates for summarizing the analyses at the three boundaries
- extend this analysis to examine interdependencies between the firm's strategic boundaries and their strategic implications

Strategic issues relevant to the firm's competitive position, we argued in Chapter 5, invariably present themselves at the boundaries of its *unique competing space*. The firm's *unique competing space*, after all, represents the core of what really matters to the firm in a competitive sense. Firms therefore need to continually monitor and scrutinize conditions as they evolve the boundaries of their *unique competing space*. Likewise, the need for any strategic response on the part of the firm is triggered by issues that present themselves at one or more of the firm's strategic boundaries. Real business contexts, however, are complex. Issues emerging at one boundary are often coupled to issues that present themselves at one or both of the other two boundaries. Hence, managers also need to look beyond any single boundary; they need to probe interactions evolving between boundaries.

Consequently, focus on the strategic boundaries enables managers to *"cut to the chase"* in terms of what really matters to the firm.

The exercise presented in the following section provides guidance on framing questions that probe the dynamics and strategic implications of change evolving at individual boundaries of the firm's unique competing space as well as interactions between issues arising at more than one of the firm's strategic boundaries.

The three sets of questions presented in the following section pertain to the boundaries indicated in Figure A1:

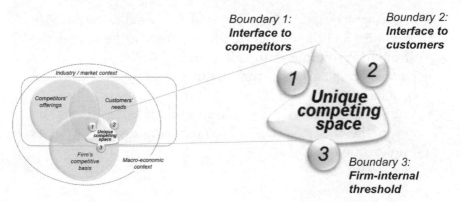

Figure A1   Strategic boundaries of the firm's *unique competing space*

> **NOTE:**
>
> The analysis approach described in this section pertains to an *individual* expression of a *unique competing space* within the firm. As argued in Chapter 4, firms typically have more than one value offering; consequently, their business activities are spread over a portfolio of *unique competing spaces* and associated *value propositions*. A *unique competing space* and associated *value proposition* can be defined for any value offering that: (1) addresses specific customers' needs; (2) draws on dedicated resources and capabilities within the firm; and that (3) competes against potential competitors' offerings. To cover the firm's business activities, the exercises described in the following sections ultimately need to be carried out for each of the firm's relevant value offerings (in practice, the 20% of the business activities that constitute 80% of its competitive impact is a good starting point); consolidated findings across the firm's portfolio of *unique competing spaces* then provide one expression of its competitive position.

Boundary 1: *The competitor interface: competitors' offerings and the competition*

Questions:

- Who are our competitors today?
- Who might they be in the foreseeable future?
- What do we know about them?
- What don't we know about them?
- What is their competitive offering?
- What do we know about their competitive offering?
- What do we know about customers' perception of our competitors' offering?
- What makes it inferior (possibly superior?) to ours?

- How is our competitors' offering changing – and in response to what?

More questions, but with a view to potential implications:

- What critical threats are emerging from our competitors?
- How quickly are these evolving?
- Which are the really critical ones; the ones requiring prioritized attention?
- How are we protecting ourselves?
- Where are we most vulnerable in view of our competitors' offering(s)?
- What new, potential opportunities are there relative to our competitors?
- How are we exploiting these?

Having addressed these (and possibly other) questions relevant to boundary "*1*", the most critical issues, threats and opportunities are summarized in the following suggested manner (Table A1):

Table A1 Summary: Competitor interface

1. THE COMPETITOR INTERFACE	
1. *The three most **critical ISSUES** at this interface (ranked)*	1.
	2.
	3.
2. *Three **critical THREATS** emanating from the competition*	1.
	2.
	3.
3. *Three **critical OPPORTUNITIES** emerging at this interface*	1.
	2.
	3.

Boundary 2: *The customer interface: customers' needs*

Questions:

- Who are our customers?
- What are their needs; how well are these understood by the customer?
- How well do *we* understand our customers and their needs?
- How are both customers and their needs changing?
- What makes us special in the eyes of our customers?
- Where have we failed in meeting customers' needs?

More questions, but with a view to potential implications:

- What makes us the supplier of choice in our customers' eyes?
- What is the nature of the relationship we are nurturing with our customers?
- How are we strengthening our preferred customer position?

Table A2 Summary: Customer interface

2. THE CUSTOMER INTERFACE	
1. The three most **CRITICAL ISSUES** at this interface (ranked)	1.
	2.
	3.
2. Three **CRITICAL THREATS** emanating at the customer interface	1.
	2.
	3.
3. Three **CRITICAL OPPORTUNITIES** emerging at the customer interface	1.
	2.
	3.

- What new opportunities are there relative to our customers?
- What entirely new, emerging customer segments might we be targeting?
- How are we exploiting these?

Boundary 3: *The firm-internal threshold*

Questions:

- What are our most critical resources/capabilities?
- To what extent are these enabling us to achieve a position of competitive advantage?
- What critical organizational factors enable us most towards achieving competitive advantage?
- Which hinder us most?

More questions, but with a view to potential implications:

- How do we orchestrate our strengths most effectively for maximum impact; what is most important in our organization for "getting our act together"?

Table A3 Summary: Firm-internal threshold

3. THE FIRM-INTERNAL THRESHOLD	
1. The three most **CRITICAL ISSUES** at this interface (ranked)	1.
	2.
	3.
2. Three **CRITICAL THREATS** that present themselves at this interface	1.
	2.
	3.
3. Three **IMPORTANT OPPORTUNITIES** that present themselves at this interface	1.
	2.
	3.

- Which critical few issues, if resolved in the way we mobilize our resources, would make a substantial difference to our competitiveness?
- What is hindering us from resolving these?
- What are the critical internal hurdles to ensure the optimal transfer of strategic resources into our unique competing space?
- How do we remove these and nurture a smooth running organization?

Consolidation of analysis findings with a reflection on implications for the firm's *unique competing space*

Finally, we pull the outcomes of the preceding boundary analyses together and present these in a table that summarizes the most critical issues, threats and opportunities for the organization's *unique competing space*.

We can now take the key findings from the preceding analyses that scope the dynamics at the boundaries of the firm's *unique competing*

Table A4 Summary analysis: The *unique competing space*

4. SUMMARY ANALYSIS: UNIQUE COMPETING SPACE	
1. The three most **CRITICAL ISSUES** *challenging our firm's* **unique competing space**	1.
	2.
	3.
2. Three **CRITICAL THREATS** *to our firm's* **unique competing space**	1.
	2.
	3.
3. Three most **IMPORTANT OPPORTUNITIES** *presenting themselves in our firm's* **unique competing space**	1.
	2.
	3.

space forward and consolidate these in a summary of implications and potential new strategic directions that emerge from these. Table A5 suggests a structured approach for capturing and presenting the consolidated outcomes:

Table A5 Consolidation of analysis findings; derivation of implications for the firm's *unique competing space*

"UNIQUE COMPETING SPACE"
("in a nutshell" for the respective value offering: ". . . the 2 or 3 factors or attributes of our value offering that really make us stand out in our customers' eyes"):

Critical OPPORTUNITY (or THREAT) *for creation (defense) of value offering associated with the unique competing space*	*Competitive implications of opportunities (or threats) for the unique competing space*
1.	
2.	
3.	

Consolidated analysis findings	
Implications for the UNIQUE COMPETING SPACE *(enhancement/defense of existing value offering)*	*Factors determining uniqueness, superiority of associated value offering*

Inter-boundary analysis: scoping linked issues

In the preceding analysis, we have focused on individual boundaries. This is always a good starting point. However, in reality, issues, threats and opportunities evolving at the boundaries of the firm's unique competing space are typically cross-boundary spanning. Strategic issues that present themselves, therefore, often lead to strategic questions that pertain to more than one boundary. Table A6 suggests issues that span two boundaries:

Table A6 Boundary spanning issues and implications

	Implications for . . .		
Perspective from . . .	**Boundary 1** *Competitor interface*	**Boundary 2** *Customer interface*	**Boundary 3** *Internal threshold*
Boundary 1 *Competitor interface*		New entrant competitors with disruptive value offerings	Sensing and interpretation of changing nature and intensity of competition; translation of these insights into appropriate responsive action
Boundary 2 *Customer interface*	Customer needs picked up and addressed by the competition		Sensing and interpretation of changing customers' needs; translation of these into appropriate responsive action
Boundary 3 *Internal threshold*	Identification of new opportunities to sustain competitive edge; alternatively, to catch up	Mobilization of internal capability to improve responsiveness to customers needs	

Issues arising at the boundaries of the firm's *unique competing space* may, however, extend to all three boundaries. In these cases, the strategic analysis needs to be extended to interdependencies between all three boundaries. As a case in point, think of the impact that *Apple*'s introduction of its *iPhone* in 2007 had on the smartphone market, and on incumbent players in the smartphone market, such as *Nokia*. From *Nokia*'s perspective, the *iPhone* represented a devastating competitive offering that emerged on its boundary "1". However, the *iPhone* also emerged as an offering that addressed customers' needs in a way that *Nokia*'s comparative offering in smartphones failed to satisfy (boundary "2"). *Nokia*'s inability to respond in a way that protected its incumbent position in the smartphone market indicates serious issues at the third boundary of its original smartphone-related *unique competing space*. Despite *Nokia*'s arguably superior technological position (*Apple* only in 2011 admitted to using *Nokia* technology in its *iPhone*, and made the first of its licensing payments), *Nokia* appears to have lost its position in the smartphone market to *Apple* as a new entrant.

Strategy Mapping and Narrative (based on Analysis of the Relevant Strategy Building Blocks)

IN APPENDIX 'B' WE:

- derive a practical approach for mapping the firm's strategy on the basis of an analysis of its relevant strategy building blocks
- extend the strategy mapping outcome to include an accompanying narrative that seeks to articulate the firm's strategy
- provide guidance on deriving an appropriate "three-minute elevator pitch" that captures and expresses the essence of the firm's strategy "in a nutshell".

Strategy Mapping

A number of approaches exist for mapping the firm's strategy.[1] Typically these are used in conjunction with strategic performance measurement and monitoring. In this section we present an approach that focuses not so much on providing a means of assessing strategic performance; rather the strategy mapping approach described in the following sections serves primarily to distill and consolidate the essence of the firm's strategy into a form that can be easily understood and communicated. It builds on the outcomes of the preceding analysis (Appendix A) in that it elaborates on the outcomes of the analysis of the firm's *unique competing space*; enhances this with an appropriate "reason to believe"; and derives an accompanying narrative that articulates the firm's strategy. The approach derived in this section draws on the strategy building blocks relevant to the firm's *unique competing space*.

Strategy mapping and the accompanying narrative are critically important for strategic thinking; in particular for communicating the essence of the firm's strategy to its multiple stakeholders. Collis and Rukstad (2008)[2] argue that few executives can summarize the essence of their firm's strategy in an articulate, concise and brief statement. In this section we show how the concepts and analysis approaches derived and presented throughout this book can be applied to achieve this critical managerial task.

Figure B1 presents the general scheme involved in developing the strategy map and accompanying narrative. The strategy building blocks in Chapter 1 serve to prompt the inputs to the underlying analysis.

---

[1] See Marr, B. (2006) *Strategic Performance Management*, Oxford: Butterworth-Heinemann/Elsevier; or Kaplan, R.S. and Norton, D.P. (2004) *Strategy Maps*, Boston: Harvard Business School Press.

[2] Collis, D.J. and Rukstad, M.G. (2008) Can You Say What Your Strategy Is? *Harvard Business Review*, April 2008, pp. 82–90.

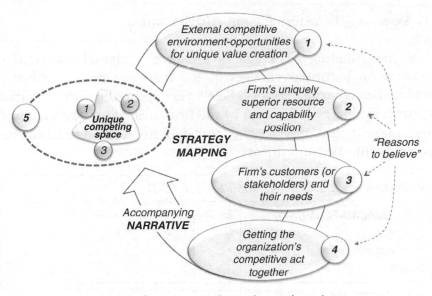

Figure B1 Strategy mapping and narrative scheme

The four building blocks probing the external context, internal basis of competitiveness, customers' needs and the organization's ability to orchestrate mobilization of its resources and capabilities in a way that makes them strategically relevant converge on the expression of the firm's *unique competing space*.

The following templates provide a structured approach to the analysis that culminates in a one-page summary of the firm's strategy.

1. Assessing the external competitive context

The first building block probes the firm's external competitive context, in particular changes in the macro-economic, industry and market contexts. Factors affecting change in the firm's external context cannot be influenced by the firm; a good understanding of them nonetheless provides critical insight into existing and emerging opportunities and threats.

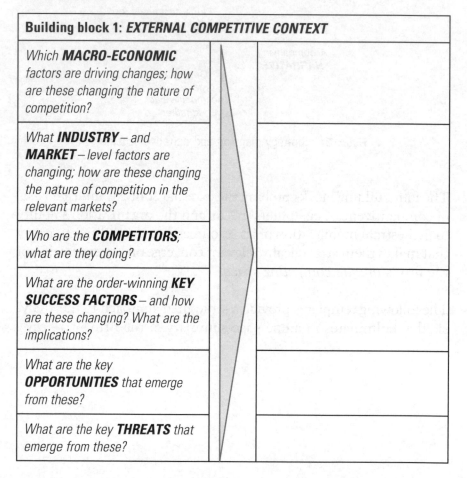

Building block 1: *EXTERNAL COMPETITIVE CONTEXT*		
Which **MACRO-ECONOMIC** factors are driving changes; how are these changing the nature of competition?		
What **INDUSTRY** – and **MARKET** – level factors are changing; how are these changing the nature of competition in the relevant markets?		
Who are the **COMPETITORS**; what are they doing?		
What are the order-winning **KEY SUCCESS FACTORS** – and how are these changing? What are the implications?		
What are the key **OPPORTUNITIES** that emerge from these?		
What are the key **THREATS** that emerge from these?		

2. Assessing the firm's internal basis of competitiveness

The second building block probes the firm's internal basis of competitiveness. These are mainly the firm's (ideally uniquely superior) resources and capabilities, and therefore those factors that the firm controls.

Building block 2: *INTERNAL BASIS OF COMPETITIVENESS*		
What are our **UNIQUE RESOURCES AND CAPABILITIES**; what makes them "unique"?		
How do our resources and capabilities compare with our competitors?		
To what extent are we exploiting our unique resources and capabilities?		
What key **OPPORTUNITIES** exist exploiting these even more?		
What **THREATS** exist with respect to our resources/capabilities?		
What are the key **THREATS** that emerge from these?		

3. Assessing the firm's customers' needs

The third building block probes the firm's customers (in an extended sense, stakeholders) and their needs, and how these are changing.

Building block 3: *CUSTOMERS' NEEDS ASSESSMENT*		
Who are our **CUSTOMERS** (and key stakeholders)?		
What are our **CUSTOMERS' NEEDS** and how are these changing?		
What is enabling us to understand our customers' needs better than our competitors?		
What new **OPPORTUNITIES** are emerging with respect to our customers?		
What **THREATS** are emerging?		

4. Assessing the firm's organizational wherewithal

The fourth building block probes the firm's ability to orchestrate its (ideally uniquely superior) resources and capabilities in a way that makes them competitively relevant. Essentially this task focuses on the mobilization of the firm's strategic resources and capabilities across the firm's internal threshold (third boundary) into the relevant *unique competing space*. Resources and capabilities in the firm are strategically relevant only when this is accomplished.

Building block 4: *GETTING THE ACT TOGETHER*		
What are our greatest **PERFORMANCE STRENGTHS?**		
What are our greatest **WEAKNESSES/ VULNERABILITIES?**		
Which few improvements would have a significant impact on our competitive performance?		
What are the key **OPPORTUNITIES** *emerging for the organization?*		
What are the key **THREATS** *facing the organization?*		

5. Pulling it all together: the firm's *unique competing space*, associated elements and strategy

This final template pulls together key elements of the preceding analyses:

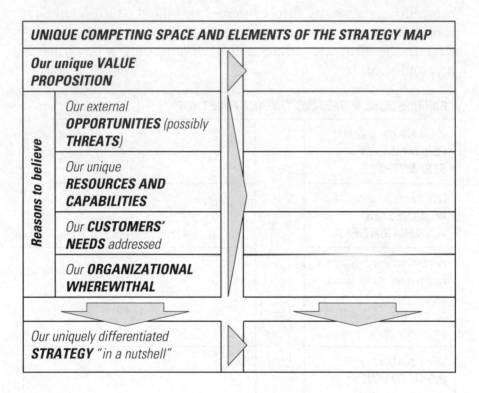

Strategy Narrative

The strategy narrative is the final piece of this exercise. It goes hand in hand with the strategy derived in the previous section. The strategy narrative summarizes in the form of a relatively short brief the essence of the strategy map. It articulates the firm's context and provides the underlying rationale for the strategy derived. Alongside a clear statement of the strategy it also provides supporting substantiation derived from the analyses of the constituent building blocks.

There is no prescription for its format and style, the strategy narrative is normally no longer than about 500 words; its storyline needs to be clear, readable and geared towards communicating the essence of the strategy in the most effective manner possible. Its ultimate version is the "3-minute elevator pitch," in which the essence of the strategy and its underlying rationale are credibly and effectively delivered in a time-limited briefing.

The potential power of compelling and well-scripted strategy narratives cannot be emphasized enough; they are the means by which firms optimally communicate and achieve buy-in with both external and internal key stakeholders.

Index

Index compiled by Indexing Specialists (UK) Ltd